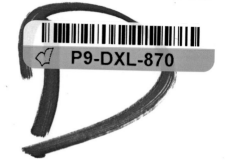

Defining Moments in
Black History

Part of the fallacy of white supremacy is the setting of whiteness as the norm and everything else as "other." Have you ever thought about the fact that even though most of this country's predominately white colleges had racial discrimination as part of their founding principles they are referred to simply as "colleges" or "universities"; however, our schools had to be specifically labeled as "black colleges and universities"? The same is true for fraternities, sororities, churches, dolls, books, and even Jesus! Black Jesus? I'm still trying to figure that one out since the Bible itself describes Jesus as a black man. Nowhere is this white standard-setting more outrageous than when it comes to history. When the topic is about anybody other than white folks, it has to be labeled: Black, Latino, Native American, etc.; but white folks have been allowed to own "history." As this planet's original people, there is no history without us. Further, even when we moved outside of Africa, from ancient Greece and Rome to the Russian Empire to the start of the American Revolution to today, black folks have touched all of humanity's most significant events. Neither the world nor America would be what they are today without the contributions of people of African Ancestry, let us be clear once and for all that black history is "history."

Defining Moments in Black History

Reading Between the Lies

DICK GREGORY

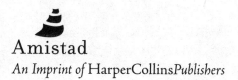

Amistad
An Imprint of HarperCollins*Publishers*

HarperCollins books may be purchased for educational, business, or sales promotional use. For information, please email the Special Markets Department at SPsales@harpercollins.com.

FIRST EDITION

Designed by Paula Russell Szafranski

Frontispiece © Chris Felver/Getty Images

Library of Congress Cataloging-in-Publication Data has been applied for.

ISBN 978-0-06-244869-9

17 18 19 20 21 LSC 10 9 8 7 6 5 4

To the women and men in the struggle.

Particularly the women.

Most people are scared of books. What I have to say to them is you can burn a book, it can't burn you.

—DICK GREGORY

Contents

Defining Moments in
Black History

Introduction: Dick·o·lo·gy

Nobody on the planet's got a better memory than a man who is illiterate. When he hits on a woman, since he can't write down her name, number, and address, he's got to *memorize* it.

I wasn't always the smartest man in the room. On October 12 they closed the schools. I thought they did it for my birthday, since I was born on that day. It made me feel special. I didn't know anything about Columbus Day when I was coming up. I'm amused by that now, but what I've come to learn in my long life is that ignorance is not bliss; it is time consuming and costly as hell.

Case in point: As a boy, I loved cowboy movies and went to see them three times a week, with the big show being on Sundays. I could relate to the cowboy because I saw my life in his. In every scene, he wore the same pair of boots, the same jacket, the same outfit. His shoes were not shined. His socks were not clean. I never saw him read a book. Never saw him go to dinner. And I said, *That's me.*

Cowboys were the biggest sensation on the planet at the time, and I thought I was one of them. But reality quickly set in. After the movie was over and I was leaving, I would walk through the alleys on my way home. I was embarrassed. Although the cowboys wore the same clothes, and that made me feel comfortable in my poverty, I was not fully affirmed because I did not see any black cowboys in the movies. Once the movie was over, I was reminded that I was a poor black boy, and I felt shame.

My boyhood shame shaped my life and my beliefs. It made me recognize that you don't buy a Rolls-Royce and go back to the ghetto with it. You hang out where Rolls-Royce people hang out. Why? Because you violate poor people with the very act of showing them what you have and reminding them of what is out of reach to them. The people in the ghetto are driving around in twenty-year-old Fords. If you bring a Rolls-Royce around, you obviously embarrass them. This is one of the reasons I'm disturbed by some black ministers, those that flash their excess around their poor congregants and claim it's a blessing from God. Why is God blessing only you? See, Catholic priests, no matter how much money they have, they all wear uniforms. No fancy clothes to make other folks feel bad about their own bargain basement clothing.

If I had a church and a Rolls-Royce, I would park six blocks away from the church and put on my robe. As I've matured, I've realized that poverty is nothing to be ashamed of. The way I see it, the poor make a sacrifice for the rich, but that's a whole other story.

Although I felt bad after seeing the cowboy movies, while I was watching them I was transported. I've never been on a horse in my life, literally. I didn't have a horse, but I'd slap my leg and say, "Giddy up, giddy up!" And when my mama made me mad, I'd say "pow" and point my finger like it was a gun.

After that, what were the odds of me growing up and liking nonviolent Martin Luther King Jr.? As a boy, John Wayne was my hero. John Wayne didn't talk about nonviolence. "If you're right and they're wrong, then kill 'em"—that's what John Wayne said, and I loved that. Then I had to rethink that whole thing when I got to know King. Now I look at John Wayne and say, *You nasty, violent, ignorant somebody.* That's why I say ignorance is not bliss, but costly. I did not understand the limits of violence. It took Martin Luther King to show me. And I didn't know that I shouldn't be ashamed of being poor either.

But change in attitude does not come quickly. When I was in high school, I worked at the Shell gas station making more money than I had ever had. One summer day, the weather was good. A few of the other guys and I were talking trash and looking at some girls who were standing on the corner. I said, "Man, let's forget about work," and we skipped work for several days to hang with the girls. We didn't worry about it until it got close to payday. At the same time, we were kind of thinking that we might be fired, since we hadn't shown up for work in days. We were scared to return. Sure enough, when we went back to work, the boss said to me, "Where you been?" I lied and said, "My mama died." Next thing I know, he came on over, started touching my shoulder, saying, "Oh, I'm so sorry to hear that. Oh, I'm just so sorry." Then he opened up his old, worn-out leather wallet, took out a ten-dollar bill, handed it to me, and said, "Just enjoy yourself." I said, "I came to get my check!" He said, "Hold on. I'll get it for you."

About six months later, same thing happened. This guy named Charles Simmons and I were just sitting outside talking trash to the girls, not thinking about going to work. Eventually, we went to get our checks, and my white employer asked, "Where you been?" I said, "My mama died." And he did the same thing as the previous time—patted me on the back and gave me money. At that moment, I knew that he was not really thinking about me. Learning that my boss did not sincerely care was an important lesson for me to learn early in life. I have not worked for anyone since. I've been on my own making up my career as I go along. People call me an activist, social critic, comedian, and, let's not forget, conspiracy theorist. In this book, I have combined all of these talents to allow us to look at American history differently. Part of my unique perspective was having been there. I was friends with most of the people mentioned and I stood next to some of them during their greatest moments— Muhammed Ali, Michael Jackson, Rosa Parks, Angela Davis, Dr. King, Malcolm X, and so many more.

Along with my activism, I have spent my entire life in the pursuit of knowledge—knowledge as it has meaning to me as a person of color. I appreciate all people, no matter their race, especially since we all evolved from the same stardust. But we must all be honest and recognize that the way black people see the world is quite different from how others see it, which is as it should be.

One's race is more clearly defined by cultural practices and values than skin color. For instance, have you ever read those stories about people who were found dead at their jobs? One of those stories where they found a person keeled over, head on his desk, and he was not discovered until the next day? I guarantee that would never be a black person. If black people feel a little bit funny, like something-ain't-right-in-the-air kind of funny, we're calling in sick. If it's looking like rain, and you know what that does to our hairdo, we're thinking of calling in. If we ate too much at dinner and our clothes are too tight the next morning, we're not going to work. Many Caucasian people, on the other hand, love their work. At their jobs they are affirmed and well-compensated. They're given all the resources they need to make every day a good day. So, it's no surprise that they love their work so much that they don't even want to retire. If I didn't work for myself, I would have retired a long time ago! I would still retire, even though I know that about a hundred years before I was born, black folks were qualified to do what I'm doing now but *they didn't get the chance.* But, seriously, other races have a different relationship to work because historically they haven't been demeaned by it—and they most definitely have not not been compensated for their labor. The earlier I got to work every day, the earlier I'd lose my dignity. And if I could find a reason to get off early, the sooner I'd get it back.

In my pursuit of knowledge, throughout my more than eighty years on this planet, I've learned many interesting things, particularly about culture. Way, way back, lightning struck a pig barn. Know how rich you need to be to keep pigs in a barn? Well, two brothers, the sons of the barn's owner, ran out to the barn and saw that it was burning down. They smelled something they liked: barbeque. They started sniffing and said, "Damn! That stuff smells *good!*" But check this out: thousands of years passed before people realized that they could cook a pig *without burning the barn down.* That's how long it takes to undo a *culture,* a way that people do things that's been there forever, because that's how they've always done it. In fact, they think they'd be crazy to do it a different way.

If your children were born in France, and then you and your wife weren't around, what language would they speak? French, right?

Language doesn't have a thing to do with human nature, with who you are as a person. It's culture. *Wars* are about culture. That's why you and I, if we live in the same country, can't have a war. The Civil War was about culture: "The North didn't want the South to have slaves."

If you go to Japan today, can you read a Japanese sign? No, you can't. You think the universal God wanted something to change when you crossed the border? You think God wanted the border to begin with? That's how the whole thing is messed up.

In relation to culture, I always say: white is not a color, it's an attitude.

Black folks—we don't appreciate ourselves. Look here: Anytime an oppressor says, "If you have one-thirty-second Negro blood, you're a nigger," I say, "Wait a minute." Think about that now. This is my enemy; this is a guy who hates me and will do anything to keep me down. So, what he is saying is that in order to equal one of me, you've got to put thirty-two white boys next to me. But black folks don't hear it that way. We hear the negative part of that statement. I mean, if you have a dollar bill, in order to equal that dollar in pennies, you'd have to have a *hundred* of those little things. It's the same with white folks and black folks. We're powerful, creative, and often ingenious. Unfortunately, there are only a handful of us who believe in our greatness. I'm not saying that other people are not exceptional. I'm saying that *we are, too*. Again, we are all from the same stardust.

If black people believed in ourselves, and not what people say about us, we would be leading the discussion on race relations rather than reacting to it. In fact, we could make the world realize how ridiculous racism is. For example, when I participated in civil rights marches, many times whites would attack us with dogs and fire hoses. At some point later, I had to laugh about the situation. Think about it: these folks were so angry that they were acting stone-cold crazy—frothing at the mouth, chasing blacks with dogs, spitting on us. And angry about what? Racism makes no sense. Whites hate blacks just because of the color of our skin. Any rational person knows that we can't control the color of our skin. But it's not our skin, it's who we *are* that makes them lose their minds. Or maybe it's seeing in our faces the atrocities they committed in our shared past?

So, now, you look at this mess we're in, this racist mess that came about because we're not thinking. Slavery has messed up our minds in countless ways. For instance, a black woman is the only woman on the planet who goes to a place called a "beauty parlor." All other women go to a hair salon. But our women have been convinced that they are not attractive. There in the beauty parlor spending good money for what God already gave them—hair, nails, lashes. I'm here to say, God made everybody, and did God make ugly people? Sears and Roebuck didn't give me nappy hair. The same universe that put the sun, the moon, and the stars in place gave me nappy hair. But then the white boy comes in and starts praising his definition of beauty in the media, and we believe it. If I was here a billion years before you, then don't tell me that stuff you're using ain't mine.

The Thirteenth, Fourteenth, and Fifteenth Amendments freed black people, made us citizens, and gave black men the right to vote (although they prevented us from doing so). The white woman didn't get the right to vote until 1921. Now, that white woman was the white boy's mama, but he would not let her vote. That was his *mama*. That was his *daughter*. That was his *wife*. That was his *girlfriend*. Anyway, we keep looking up to the white man, saying to ourselves, *Oh, I'd like to be like him*. For so many of us, our minds are so messed up that we want to be like him even though it does not make cultural sense.

Meanwhile, he's trying to be like *us*, except we don't know it because he's trying to keep us from seeing that's what he's doing. People say, "Well, I don't know why these white folks are lying in the sun trying to get a suntan." Man, hear what he's saying: a suntan, not a sun*black*. (I was doing some research and found an article that said that 80 percent of the coral reefs had been destroyed by suntan lotion. They've been there trillions of years, and if suntan lotion does that to a coral reef, what do you think it's doing to people? The universe will pay your ass back.) A white man may not *say* he's trying to be like us, but look at what he's *doing*. A rose by any other name, see what I'm saying?

We don't appreciate ourselves. We don't appreciate what it means to go through what black people've been through and still be here. Think about being under stress all the time and what that does to your body—the adrenaline rush and all the other physiological stuff. Did you ever walk down the street and see a cat turn the corner and come up on a dog? Ever see what happens to the cat's body? It goes straight up. That's the response that God gave it: fight or flight. Hair sticks up, shoots out every which way, like the Big Bang if the universe were made of fur. It's the same with humans and adrenaline. Your eyes—suddenly you can see forty miles away. The fastest animal out there—you can outrun it. You have the energy of you and somebody else, too. Now, that's meant to happen for just a few minutes, until you're out of danger. That fight-or-flight response wasn't meant to exist twenty-four hours a day, every day. But when something that's supposed to last a few minutes happens to you *all the time*, how do you think that will mess you up? Why do you think black folks have high blood pressure so bad (that and pork rinds)? It's a genetic response to the oppression we've been dealing with for four hundred years, passed down from one generation to the next.

If I were to leave home and go to work knowing a racist was there, I would start getting scared. But I can't quit my job. Now, that's not a problem for just black folks. Most other folks can't quit their jobs, either. They've got mortgages to pay; they've got children to send to college. Financial worries are the same with black folks, except we also have to be worried about racism, too. I have to go to work, I have to take care of this, take care of that, just like white folks, but with all that *pressure* I feel, that fight-or-flight response, that suppressed fear and rage—it changes my whole body chemistry. When I leave work and yell at my wife or children, it's not because I'm mad at *them*. I'm mad at the boss man, but it would cost me my job to say something to him. If I haul off and slap him upside the head, the rest of the Negroes say, "Nigger must be crazy. He knew he was going to be fired."

That's why, when black folks go to church, our music has got to be loud. (Go to a white Catholic church; they're not hollering.) Our music's got to be loud just so we can forget the boss man and the week we just had, so we can have a little bit of *peace*. We've got to un-mess up our minds from what we've been through. We use the music to clear our heads, and we move our bodies in dance to shake off the excess stress.

So, if the white boy thinks it takes thirty-two of him to equal one of me, that's why.

As I said, we don't appreciate ourselves. We believe what other folks say about us. The purpose of this book is to spread the knowledge, to get the world thinking again, and to see what is truly there and not just take what we are told as truth. When I was a little boy, maybe my mama didn't read that well, but we had every encyclopedia you could find. I would blow the dust off of them and read a volume every now and again.

Valuing information is something I have passed on to my children. Most of us do that. But, keep in mind, your children don't hear what you mean; they hear what you *say*. So, when you teach your black children, "You've got to work twice as hard as a white child," they hear you saying they're dumb.

One day, my then-eight-year-old son Christian said to his

mother, "I want to tell you something, but don't tell Dad. I was out for recess and I forgot I left something behind and went back into the school to get it. I overheard a white teacher say, 'Christian's so dumb sometimes I think he is not a Gregory.'"

When I came home that night, Lillian, my wife, told me about the situation. I went in to see Christian. "Dad, am I as dumb as they say?" he asked me. And I said, "You are a dumb little boy. That's what you are. Your mama won't tell you that. Okay? But *I'll* tell you because you are, and I'll tell you because the difference between As and Ds has got nothing to do with smartness! It's *discipline*, that's all. And your sister Michelle—my advice is to follow her around everywhere she goes and do what she does."

One day when Christian was thirteen years old, I was running through the house getting ready to go out, and he stopped me and said, "How did you know if I started following Michelle I'd start making straight As?" And I said, "The difference between an A and an F is discipline, and your sister is the most disciplined person I know." Today Christian is a doctor.

It's true. I did not have any issues with my daughters when it came to education. Most boys spend time playing. Girls make better grades because they are in the house studying. For the most part, that's the way black girls are raised—to stay in the house.

One day, my daughter Michelle came to me and said, "Well, now, since you made me go to this white school, I'm fixing to go to grad school. Where should I go?" Since she was acting so high and mighty, I said, "Go to the London School of Economics." She did not even know it existed when I mentioned it, but a few months later she came to me with an acceptance letter. Today, she has the only PhD in sexual harassment in the workplace on the whole planet. If she comes in and testifies against you as an expert witness, that's it— you're going down, because she's the authority on the subject.

We can get into serious trouble by not valuing education and learning. Did you know that 98 percent of the children who drown in the summertime are black? Why? Because historically we weren't allowed in swimming pools because of Jim Crow. That law put a bad taste in black folks' mouths, and to this day I don't know how to swim. On my family's farm, there was a lake a thousand feet deep. I told her, if one of our kids starts to drown, *you* go get him. I'm not going in the water. I can't swim. I'm not going to *play* like I'm swimming. And when I was home, and the kids were out in the water playing, I would leave the house. I didn't even want to hear them call my name when they were near the water.

EVERYBODY KNOWS WE WERE AT ONE TIME ENSLAVED, but many of us think that we're *supposed* to be slaves, and act like we believe it, too. Look here: when Africans were brought to the Americas, we didn't become slaves until we got here. If you jumped off the ship, you weren't a slave; you were a person who had been kidnapped. You didn't pick cotton on the way over here. It's not in your *nature* to be a slave.

These people we're dealing with didn't raid a country; they raided a whole continent. I'm from a whole *continent*, a continent made up of tribes at war with one another. The Oyos didn't like the Dahomeys, who didn't like the so-and-sos, who didn't like the so-and-sos. We black folks had spears, and for a thousand years we were throwing them at *one another*. In that way, we were like the people in Europe who were also fighting one another, although they used different weapons. Europe is a continent. Almost every single one of those countries on that continent has fought every last one of the others. They didn't have to fight Asia; they were too busy fighting each other all over the continent.

Now, in slavery times, black folks were put on ships in West

Africa. That very same spot where the slaves were put on ships is where hurricanes start. Most hurricanes start in West Africa and follow the same trail that the slave ships followed. There is no record of a hurricane hitting America before that. If you don't believe me, look it up. The first Africans were brought to America as slaves in 1619. The first hurricane slammed into this place in 1635. I say a hurricane is the spirit of a black woman. (That's why it starts with *her*!) No slave was offloaded until the ships got to the Caribbean. Hurricanes stay below water until they get all the way to the Caribbean. They will hit the United States and come up the East Coast, all the way to Maine. Now, Canada is as close to Maine as a car is to the curb, but Canada doesn't have hurricanes half as bad as we have. Why not? Because Canada never messed with a black woman like we did, although they did have slaves.

That black sister, she's the only person on this planet who can take a butter knife and cut your tires to the rim. And everybody says, "Wait a minute. A *butter* knife?" Better believe it, man. That is who she is. That's who *we* are. That's that spirit. That's power.

Other folks see it, but we don't.

Here's another indication of our power in the universe. Prior to the Middle Passage sharks had a natural migration. They swam in this particular pattern for hundreds of years. Then the Middle Passage comes along—all that blood in the ocean. The blood of millions of black people. The sharks changed their migration pattern to follow the blood. They continue to swim along that same route today. Slavery was wrong on so many levels that it changed the world in ways we do not even recognize.

That's our power.

You know what you can do? Learn what black folks have already done, and understand how smart and tough you needed to be to survive back then and now. Black folks are superheroes. We can be invisible when we have to be.

Think about your mama's mama: maybe she was a maid for white folks. Now, how many times have you been in a cab and started talking to your friend like the cab driver can't hear a thing? It was the same with your mama's mama, listening to white folks who forgot she was in the room. It was the same thing when the black folks worked at the hospital where they took Martin Luther King Jr. after he was shot on the balcony in Memphis. When they took him to the hospital, he was still alive—which is what the black people who worked there at the time told me. They said that as he lay on that gurney, King was spat on and then smothered to death. Our invisibility is part of our survival. We can even transform into cowboys, despite the fact that there was no evidence of a black cowboy back when I used to watch cowboys on TV. We got so we knew white folks—we had to, just to survive.

Now it's time to know ourselves. It's time to *value* ourselves. Give you one example: I can't understand how Negroes, with all the humiliation we've been through, would join a black group, a fraternity, that would paddle their asses. We come from a history of humiliation. The white mob that was ready to do all kinds of crazy stuff to you and me—the folks in that mob didn't paddle one another's asses so they could be in the mob. So why would you do that to somebody who looks like you? And why would you up and *volunteer* to have somebody do that to you?

The thing is when you go outside this messed-up country, everybody else in this messed-up world thinks we're beautiful. Check this out: I used to go to Russia all the time. I took my wife, Lil, with me once. The subways in Russia go three miles down—so far down in the earth you think you're about to come out the other side. And clean? They're cleaner than any hospital you've got in

America, or any restaurant, cleaner than anything you ever *saw* over here. Anyway, we're on the subway, and people are looking at Lil. One of them comes up and stares right at her. And Lil looks at me and says, "Thirty million Russians ride the subway every day in Moscow. They're not doing this to one another. I can't believe you let these white folks do me like this." And I said, "Yeah? The day I'll stand up for your honor it won't be around thirty million Russians. The odds've got to be a little better than that."

Then I thought of something, and said, "I've been coming over here five years and they ain't never looked at *me* like that." Then I figured it out. I said, "The Russians had seen black American men all over the world as soldiers but have never seen a black woman— and *now they know how beautiful you are.* That's what they're looking at, the way a child looks at a Christmas toy. That's who you *are.* I can't see it, because a white racist system told me you ain't nothing beautiful. I can't see it because they told me, 'Your skin was too black and your hair was too nappy.'"

Beauty is what the *real* world sees when they look at a black woman. It's what it sees when it looks at Lil. It's what it sees when it looks at Michelle Obama, Halle Berry, and Fannie Lou Hamer. (Do not let me get started on fine women.) Beauty—that's what the *real* world sees.

"I don't see it," I told Lil, "because these white folks done told me how ugly you are, with them big lips and big nose and all that."

Think about that, now. For almost fifty years, the Russian people stood toe to toe with the United States of America in the Cold War; that's how tough and smart those people were. You hear me? And *they're* staring at my wife because she's beautiful. So, that's the whole game of it. They see what we black folks don't see, what we need to start seeing.

Know who you are. Value who you are. Knowing yourself and valuing yourself comes from knowing what's true and accurate. I went to Iran in the 1970s, when the Ayatollah Khomeini was in charge, kicking America's ass. He sent his secretary, a man, to tell me that I had to leave the country that weekend because Iran had word they were going to be hit by a surprise attack from Iraq. Before I left, Khomeini sent me a long letter, thanking me for being there. He wrote, "You are beautiful, Uncle Tom." Now, I had enough sense to know that the admiration he had for me was real. It was due to my own ignorance that I didn't know who Uncle Tom really was. One brother will call another one "Uncle Tom" like it's the worst insult he can pull out of his whole nappy head, not realizing that the original Uncle Tom was a hero who defied his master. Don't believe me? Go read the book *Uncle Tom's Cabin*. Uncle Tom was based on a real person, Josiah Henson. He rescued 118 black folks from slavery.

I remember when I was a little boy, I heard the old black folks say, "There's some people in Africa that white folks ain't never messed with, and they're not *going* to mess with, because they control everything." They said, "Those people are the Uncle Toms, the shape shifters." I just thought that meant that black folks could get real mean, not that they could change into gorillas or elephants or something crazy like that. But, in a way, shape shifters are what we are because black folks make ourselves into whatever we need to be to survive.

Think about Napoleon. That short little French dude set out to conquer the world, and damn near did it, too. He had the single greatest military capability in the history of the planet at that time, had all of Europe trembling while he conquered territory right and left. Then he went to the Americas. That was the first time that little dude messed up, because it was the first time he messed with

black folks. The black general Toussaint L'Ouverture—now that
was one smart man—had already led a slave revolt and taken over
the French colony in Saint-Domingue, which is now Haiti. Napoleon decided he wanted the land back. He and his gang managed to
trick Toussaint L'Ouverture, who died in a French prison, but the
rest of the black folks there gave the French troops such a fit that
Napoleon finally said, "Later for this. We're out of here"—except it
sounded nicer than that because he said it in French—and he left.
Pulled out of the Americas, signed the Louisiana Purchase, and
went the hell on back to France and didn't look back. All because
of what happened when he decided to mess with black people. You
hear what I'm trying to say? That's the power we have when we're
together, when we do what we need to do. That's why we need to
celebrate ourselves.

We did that by *ourselves*. Nobody gave Toussaint L'Ouverture
and his soldiers any help. Many folks think that all blacks live off
the system, but most of the time we keep surviving without anybody or anything except *ourselves*. Look at when Franklin Delano
Roosevelt was president, during the Great Depression. Roosevelt
said, "Let's create the WPA," the Works Progress Administration,
which was meant to put white folks to work so they could earn
a decent living. So, now here's a white boy at the WPA digging
a hole that doesn't need to be dug; his brother comes along that
evening and fills it back up. Anyway, black folks weren't included.
Yet, we praise Roosevelt. Black folks didn't get included in Social
Security, either—not the way it worked then, at least. Social Security initially didn't cover farmers and domestics, which is what 99
percent of black folks were at the time.

Consequently, now all these black folks are out of work. How
are we going deal with it? We survived—you doing for me, me
doing for you. Maybe I don't have the money to pay you for fixing

my roof, but here are some jars of peaches. Or let me watch your children while you go to work. That's who I am. That's who you are. That's how we got by.

In the history of the planet, nobody else went through what we as black people have been through and survived. That takes strength, smarts, and spirit. And other people see it, even the ones who don't want to admit it. That's why white folks have us take care of their children. Yes, half the time we raise their damn children *for* them. That's what they see in me that I don't see in me, that holy spirit. And then they try to tell me that I ain't nothing. They know. Consider this a minute: what German would hire a Jew to take care of his house? He'd sooner burn it to the ground. And I don't know a single black person who would hire a white person to take care of their child. But white folks go all over the world and leave my mama back there to feed their children and take care of them, dress them for school. That's what I'm trying to say. If you miss that, then you miss who we are.

We feed them, take care of them. They are not dealing with slaves. They are dealing with people with no bitterness at all. That is who I am, not just some slave they brought over. The sooner we understand what we are made of, the better off we'll be.

IN THIS BOOK, I'M OFFERING INFORMATION ON A VARIETY of subjects and personalities that have influenced the world in a special way. Most of the stories come to me from my having been there. I marched in Selma during the civil rights movement, organized student rallies to protest the Vietnam War, sat in at rallies for Native American and feminist rights, and fought apartheid in South Africa. I've also been to some incredible places and have met some amazing leaders along the way.

I used to hang out with Congressman Adam Clayton Powell Jr. in Bimini. (In Bimini, they have no hotels, no buildings, just one bar that's about a mile long. All the big folks from around the world went there on their planes or yachts and drank all day. The playwright Tennessee Williams, the writer Ernest Hemingway, the actress Judy Garland, and more—that's where they used to hang out. When I went there with Adam, man, I could not believe it.) They loved Adam there. I mean wow, man, just the number one preacher in New York.

I have been to see the Taj Mahal and the rest of that stuff in India. When I came back, people asked me, "Greg, Greg. Tell me, what was it like?" I said, "I'm going to disappoint you, baby, but what I found out when I got there is the way I used to feel at home when I had five caramels in one pocket, six in the other, and a pocketful of marbles. It's the kind of place where if you don't bring it with you, it won't be there when you get there."

In 1968, I did a film with the writer James Baldwin, *Baldwin's Nigger*. Baldwin was so brilliant. I would just sit and laugh and talk with him for long periods of time. He was like something God had just spat out. It was like God told him, "You go down there, you'll have some problems, but just keep doing it." A thousand years from now they'll still be reading what Baldwin wrote—and it will still be relevant then. But his writing doesn't let you know what a funny man he was.

In addition to these incredible experiences, I've also been to jail. Anybody trying to change a country for the better (or by simply being a black man on a sunny day) is usually arrested—par for the course. I went to jail on nine counts, for nine months total, for protesting. Jail is not pleasant under any circumstances, but I tried to make the best of it. They put me off in a private room because they knew I might stir up trouble, another protest or something right inside the jail. There were bunk beds in my room. I took the bottom bunk and attached my book on meditation to the bunk above me to allow me to read hands-free. There's not a lot to do in jail, so I meditated for a long while. Next thing I knew, I heard a knocking sound. It was my head hitting the top bunk. I must have been going at it a while because there was blood on my forehead. After my body returned to the mattress, I said, "Oh, *that's* what meditation's about." *Levitation.* Several people witnessed my levitation. It's the fastest way to get out of jail, I'll tell you that!

Self-knowledge and cultural pride can also give you a feeling of levitation.

1

Searching for Freedom

It was in the *New York Times* that there are 1.5 million black men missing. They are not in jail. I couldn't imagine where they were until I saw the movie *Get Out*.

Everyone knows that slavery wasn't right. Not just human slavery, but all forms of slavery are wrong. Folks that own dogs and cats and other animals should recognize that they are practicing a form of slavery. Every time we go to the zoo, we condone slavery. The same universal God that made me and you also made dogs, cats, elephants, and gorillas. Straight up. When you own a dog, you determine when it's going to mate, when it's going to pee, when it's going to eat, when it's going to take a crap. You have to see that's slavery, because once you start off with the idea of something as being beneath you, you're lost. I tell people, you'll find out on Judgment Day. You'll see a slave master, and you will all be in the same room waiting to get that train to hell.

When you submit to another human being and let him do something to you, that violates God, violates the universe. During the slave trade, hundreds of thousands of Africans jumped off the ships carrying them and died. Our revolts against slavery are what I like to focus on, as well as the ways slavery psychologically impacted all of society. Think about it: somebody comes over to where you're living, someone you've never seen, because most of you have never seen white folks. They've come there to steal your children and to send you, the dad, to one place, the mama someplace else, and the brother yet someplace else.

During slavery, the women were of equal value to the men. Listen, there isn't another man in the world, besides the black man, who looks at his woman and says, "I'm going to get some of that booty." Have you ever heard that word used referring to a woman of another race? You know what it means? The loot the pirate takes off the ship is called booty. So, this woman, who's never been liberated—we call what she has "booty." I believe this is a direct result of slavery.

We arrive in a new land. The people in America do not speak my tongue and they do not practice my religion. Today people laugh at me and want to know why I speak English so bad. Because when the whites brought me here I wasn't speaking anything but pure Swahili. That's why. They should not try to embarrass me.

The same God that made the sun made me. I went and looked at all the Seven Wonders of the World, and I came back and I said, "Wow, none of them was made by God." How come the ocean isn't one?

I went to Egypt. A man there told me that Egypt has the third-largest tourist economy in the world. Everybody comes to see the pyramids. So, the Egyptian said, "I'd like for you and your friend to join us tonight where the superrich go, to sleep under the pyramid." I said, "Man, look at this here." I pointed at my nose. "*That's* the pyramid, you understand? And as long as I sleep on my back, I get a thousand times more energy than I'd get from that mess you're selling. My nose is my pyramid." God made it.

The Middle Passage

Slavery in America didn't start with black folks. In the 1500s, people from Spain and Portugal were over here enslaving Indians. That's what they called the natives living here, Indians, because when that dummy Christopher Columbus came here, this fool gets lost and all of a sudden he done "discovered" something. He thought he had reached India, and the mistake stuck. So, they took those poor "Indians" from their homes and sent them every which way to work in mines and fields in the Caribbean, Peru, and Panama—the ones who hadn't already died from being exposed to European germs, that is. Then word got back to the king of Spain, Charles V, about how bad the "Indians" were being treated, and he outlawed slavery in the so-called New World. (Of course, it wasn't new to the people who had been living there!) Too bad Charles waited until *after* most of the natives had been worked to death or died of disease, huh? Plus, Charles didn't have control over what the other European countries did. Even after Spain backed off, Portugal was still in the game, and then the Dutch got involved, and then—watch out—there came the English. When the English started setting up colonies over here in the Americas, in the 1600s, let me tell you, that was bad news for black folks. The English wanted slaves, too. For a while they used poor white folks from back home as what they called indentured servants, but that didn't work out too well, because they had to honor the servants' contracts, or else the servants ran away, and because the servants were white, they could blend right in wherever they went. Guess who couldn't blend in? And so, the English and other countries soon set their sights on Africans, and the slave business was on for real.

Now, the Middle Passage—that's what they called the trip

that brought slaves by ship from Africa to the Americas. Think for a second about why it's called the Middle Passage. For something to be in the middle, it's got to be between two other things. And those two other things tell you what the whole deal was really about.

The Middle Passage was the *second* leg of the journey. The first leg started in Europe. Folks from countries like Spain and Portugal, but also England and France—the same folks we think of today when we think of grace, style, and good manners—they went to Africa and traded some cheap mess they had made for live Africans. (Notice I didn't say "slaves." We weren't slaves till we got *here*.) Then, on the Middle Passage, they brought the Africans to America and the Caribbean and traded these living, breathing people (or, rather, the ones who *were* still living and breathing) to white folks here for stuff they could take back with them to Europe. The third leg of the journey was the trip back across the ocean to the homes of those dainty, graceful, civilized, slave-trading European bastards.

The main word here is *trading*. That's what the whole thing was about. The people who started the slave trade didn't hate Africans, didn't hate black folks. They didn't care about us one way or another—until they realized they could make money by capturing us and selling us as free labor. It was when the Africans got *here* and became American black folks that the real hating started. To justify keeping somebody as a slave, you've got to say—and you've got to believe it—that that person is not a real human. And the more human people seem to you, the more you've got to tell yourself they're not. If whites had admitted to themselves that they could treat other humans in such a horrible manner, it would have meant admitting that they themselves had a problem acting like human beings. So, their questioning our humanity had more to do with them than with us. One of the reasons that racism doesn't end is because we're seen as a commodity, not as human beings.

You know and I know that the Africans brought over here on those slave ships were as human as anybody else. That's what makes thinking about what our ancestors endured during the Middle Passage so horrible. But we need to think about it, because it's our history.

Think about the last time you were on a bus or subway car on a hot summer day when the air conditioner wasn't working. You're squeezed in like socks in a drawer fresh from the laundry, except *fresh* is not the right word—the man in front of you is sweating like a farmer, the man behind you smells like he took a bath in pig manure—and pretty soon you get to sweating and smelling your own self. Now imagine that instead of sitting or standing up, you're all lying down. Imagine that instead of just starting and stopping, like a bus or subway usually does, this thing you're on rises and falls like a roller coaster, making you sick to your stomach. And imagine that your stop never seems to come. An hour passes, a day, a week, two weeks—but your stop still doesn't come. Then, when it does come, you can't get off, because you're shackled to the man next to you. Maybe you start talking to each other; pretty soon you're both crying, because neither one of you knows where you're going, or what's going to happen when you get there, or whether you'll ever see your wife or son or daughter or mother or brother again. Then you notice that you've been doing all the talking, and it's been a while since your new friend said anything. Maybe he's sleeping. Then you realize that, no, he's not sleeping. He's dead. Now you're really crying, or you would be, except the odor down there has gotten so bad that you start to vomit instead. Now there's vomit all over you and nothing in your stomach, and you don't know if there's ever going to *be* anything in your stomach, because the people who brought you here haven't said a word about feeding you.

Now they do bring you some food, because you have to be healthy enough to be sold. But even if it weren't disgusting, which it is, you feel too sick to eat it. You eat anyway, because you've got to stay alive. That's the only thing you know: you've got to stay alive.

It sounds like a nightmare the way I'm describing it, but real people went through that nightmare. Millions of real people—your ancestors and mine. Are you African American? Go back enough generations in your family, and there's somebody on one of those slave ships who went through what I've just told you about. Somebody just as real as your mama—probably looked something like her, too, and for good reason. Somebody just as real as you. Think about that for a minute. Now, how do you feel?

Money and Slavery

When it comes to slavery, what people don't think about is this: most people who were buying slaves didn't have big money to buy them by the thousands. So, who put me on the boat and brought me here? It was the big-money folks. There was another group that sold slaves like somebody today sells cars. Let's say you and your brother have a car dealership; you buy the cars from the automaker, and I come and buy them from you. The bankers lend you the money to get the cars from General Motors. You pay for the cars, then you sell one to me. Slavery was like that. One guy bought slaves and sold them to another guy. But the part that's left out is: whom did the first guy buy them *from*? Who was the General Motors of the slave trade?

For that, you've got to go to Europe: Portugal, England, France, and the Netherlands. They're the ones who came up with the idea. They're the ones who explored the routes to Africa, who bought the slaves from West Africa or else just took them, and who then went from there to the Americas. They were the ones to make the first profits.

The Americans who bought the slaves made a profit, too, because they turned around and sold them. The ones they sold them to also made a profit, because the slaves did their work for free. But the *real* profits made in America off slavery went other places. Banks handled the money from slave profits, and slave owners paid insurance companies in case something happened to the slaves. And money men in the North made a fortune by investing in those banks and insurance companies. In other words, the wealth of America was built on *our* backs.

Many of those companies are still around: J.P. Morgan, New York Life, Aetna, Lehman Brothers, and a whole lot more. Their money has been passed down from generation to generation of white descendants, and people are born into those families with wealth they didn't do a thing to earn. That's where real white guilt comes from. Meanwhile, you and I are born without a pot to piss in or a window to throw it out of.

Tell that to the next person who asks you, "Slavery's been over for a hundred fifty years. How come black people still don't have anything? What's *wrong* with you?"

The continuing inequality can make us angry sometimes. Let's not take it out on one another and our community. We need to struggle together, not against each other.

Nat Turner's Revolt

Here's an example of how a white racist system can take something we ought to be proud of and turn it against us, use it to mess up our minds.

Now, believe me, I'm not taking anything away from Nat
Turner. More people should name their children Nat Turner
instead of naming them after football players. Today, a hundred
fifty-some years after the end of slavery, some black folks' minds
are still messed up, but it's not our fault. Anybody's mind would
be off if all they heard for hundreds of years was that they were
nothing. But Nat Turner? That man was *living* in slavery but he
didn't take his cues from the oppressor. He was born and enslaved
in Virginia in 1800, and slavery was all he knew. Yet he was able
to see that that wasn't how it was supposed to be. He was able to
resist what racists told him, because he was in touch with a higher
power, or he thought he was, which I guess added up to the same
thing.

The thing about Nat Turner was, from the time he was a little
boy, people around him, black and white, saw that he was special.
They figured he was going to do something great one day, even
if he *was* a slave. (If the white folks had known what that "something" was, they probably would have killed him right then and
there.) The man who owned him even gave him a Bible, which
Nat loved. Also, his mother encouraged him because she thought
he had so much potential.

Later, Nat and his mama got sold together. After their new
owner died—Nat was married by that time—Nat's wife got sold
away. That didn't sit right with Nat. Matter of fact, that might
have been the thing that pushed him to do what he did. He was
still religious, but he wasn't the turn-the-other-cheek kind of religious. More like the I-am-God's-instrument kind. He started
praying and having visions, and everything he saw pointed to
fighting against slavery. And when I say "fight," I don't mean
"protest."

He looked to the heavens for signs. On February 12, 1831, he saw a solar eclipse and took it as a sign that it was time to free his people. At first, he planned the revolt for July 4. Isn't that something? That would have been Independence Day, all right! Then he got sick, so he waited for another sign. One day in August, the sun turned a strange blue-green color, or so Turner thought it did, and that was the sign he was looking for. He planned the revolt for August 21 and started organizing. He met secretly with just a few others at first. Before they were done, their number grew to about seventy—slaves and free blacks alike.

The revolt started with Turner's master, Joseph Travis, and his family. Turner and his followers killed them all. Then they moved on to other families, and by the next day they had killed sixty whites. They wouldn't have stopped there, but then came the federal troops. Turner and the others didn't go down without a fight, though. More than a hundred slaves died, which is more than the number of white folks they killed, but the white folks left alive didn't forget the uprising, you can believe that. They were scared out of their minds. They captured Turner on October 30 and killed him on November 11. Today we celebrate Veterans' Day on November 11, but next time it's Veterans' Day, think about Nat Turner. He sacrificed as much for his people as anybody wearing the uniform of the U.S. military.

Everybody talks about Nat Turner, even those who don't know exactly what he did. And that's the problem. When people talk about slave revolts, his is the only name you hear. White folks would have you think that in almost two hundred fifty years of slavery, there was only one brotha with enough balls to say, "I'm going to be free or die trying." As if every other slave who ever lived was either happy to be picking cotton and saying "yassuh" seven hundred times a day or too scared to do a thing about it.

The truth is, there were a *lot* of slave revolts. For one thing, before Nat Turner, there was Denmark Vesey. He was a free black man—he bought his freedom in 1800 and then worked as a carpenter in South Carolina. Made a good living, too. But he wasn't satisfied being free when other black folks were still under the lash. So, he organized a revolt. You don't hear as much about Vesey as you do Nat Turner because Vesey's rebellion got uncovered before it could take place. But Vesey and his crew were *serious*. They collected more than five hundred daggers, bayonets, and spears. They would have used them, too, but whites got wind of what was happening and that was the end of that. Vesey and others were executed.

After Vesey and Turner, the revolts kept up. In 1835, whites hanged a bunch of slaves and whipped others to death because they were about to rebel. In 1853, in South Carolina, twenty-five hundred slaves got ready to fight, but one free black man informed on them.

A whole lot of black folks resisted slavery. Ever heard of Maroons? They were slaves who ran away, formed groups, and lived together. Some of them had been captured in Africa and put on ships but ran away as soon as they reached America; a lot of them even tried to get back home. In 1856, a group of Maroons terrorized whites in a couple of counties in North Carolina. Whites got so scared and nervous, in fact, that they didn't know what to do. Some of them stopped sleeping—they just stayed up all night waiting for black people to try something else. The revolts I'm telling you about—these are just the ones somebody saw fit to write down. Nobody knows how many more there were.

Vesey, Turner, and the Maroons were the blacks who took up arms. Other blacks fought slavery in other ways. Take a look at a piece of writing published in 1829 by a black man named David Walker, called the *Appeal*. Walker was a free black man who wanted other blacks to be free, too, by killing their masters if need be. (As Malcolm X would have said: *By any means necessary.*) Take a look at what Walker wrote: "[T]hey want us for their slaves, and think nothing of murdering us. . . . [A]nd believe this, that it is no more harm for you to kill a man who is trying to kill you, than it is for you to take a drink of water when thirsty." You hear what he was saying?

Don't let anybody tell you black folks were slaves because we were happy that way. Happy folks don't take up arms. *We* took up arms.

Frederick Douglass

I want you to check out something that Frederick Douglass wrote in *Narrative of the Life of Frederick Douglass*:

[S]laves are like other people, and imbibe prejudices quite common to others. They think their own better than that of others. Many, under the influence of this prejudice, think their own masters are better than the masters of other slaves; and this, too, in some cases, when the very reverse is true. Indeed, it is not uncommon for slaves even to fall out and quarrel among themselves about the relative goodness of their masters, each contending for the superior goodness of his own over that of the others. . . . It was so on our plantation. When Colonel Lloyd's slaves met the slaves of Jacob Jepson, they seldom parted without a quarrel about their masters; Colonel Lloyd's slaves contending that he was the richest, and Mr. Jepson's slaves that he was the smartest, and most of a man. Colonel Lloyd's slaves would boast his ability to buy and sell Jacob Jepson. Mr. Jepson's slaves would boast his ability to whip Colonel Lloyd. These quarrels would almost always end in a fight between the parties, and those that whipped were supposed to have gained the point at issue. They seemed to think that the greatness of their masters was transferable to themselves. It was considered as being bad enough to be a slave; but to be a poor man's slave was deemed a disgrace indeed!

What my man Frederick Douglass is saying here is some heavy stuff. It just goes to show you that as much as slavery messed up people's bodies, it messed up their minds even more. It was bad enough that black people had to work for nothing for Colonel Lloyd, Jacob Jepson, and thousands of other evil men just like them. It was bad enough that we got whipped and sold away from our parents and children and husbands and wives. It was bad enough that our lives were not our own. But what's worse than that is the slaves who *identified with their masters*, as if the slaves' value as human beings depended on what the masters were like. What they were like was *evil*! They were called "masters" because they *owned human beings*! And we slaves were ready to fight *each other* over which of the lowdown filthy dogs who owned us was the best! But it wasn't the slaves' fault. Like Douglass wrote, slaves are like other people. When you think about it, it's a wonder more black folks didn't fight with one another instead of fighting against the white man the way Denmark Vesey, Nat Turner, David Walker, and a whole lot of others did.

While you're busy shaking your head over some dumb slaves, ask yourself this: are we any better today? Black people put on the uniform of the U.S. military, our masters, and go to Vietnam, Iraq, Afghanistan, and anywhere else Uncle Sam tells us to go, and fight and kill yellow-skinned folks and brown-skinned folks on behalf of the United States, our masters—just like slaves fighting other slaves. Meanwhile, back home, one out of every half-dozen blacks is locked up for committing the same drug crimes as white dudes who walk around free. What's wrong with *that* picture? Then you've got blacks in police uniforms out there arresting other innocent blacks.

Blacks in America really need to study the Jews in Germany. Those Jews never thought they were part of Hitler's system, most of them never sided with the people oppressing them. We do. We go to war. What kind of abomination is that? How many blacks go to war because we can't find a job, and are willing to kill or be killed just so we can feed ourselves and our families?

Getting back to Frederick Douglass, it's like he said: Slaves are like other people. Too many of us have that slave mentality. It can take a lot to get past that, but a lot of us have, and Frederick Douglass was one.

He was born into slavery 1818 in Maryland. He wasn't with his mother long enough to remember her very well, and the only thing he knew about his father was that he may have been the man who owned him.

Douglass shows what you can accomplish when your mind is free. He was somewhat free. He was taught to read when he was eight years old, by one of his owners, a white lady. What he didn't learn from her, he picked up himself, sometimes by tricking white boys into showing him how to read and write words. When he got a little bit older, his rebelliousness came to the surface. Most teenagers start to rebel, but Douglass was one teenager with something to rebel *against*. He got a hold of some antislavery writings, and that fed his anger even more. Soon this got to be too much for his owner, who sent him to another plantation so they could break him. That only made Douglass more determined. A slave driver,

Mr. Covey, beat him one day till he was covered in blood. But the next time he tried to lay a hand on him, he had a fight on his hands. It lasted a good couple of hours. This time, Covey was the one doing the bleeding. He never came near Douglass again. As Douglass wrote in his *Narrative*, "This battle with Mr. Covey was the turning-point in my career as a slave." ("Career as a slave"—that cracks me up. Fred had a sense of humor.) Books say he escaped from slavery in 1838, when he was twenty, using seaman's papers he had borrowed, then gave lectures for money for the Massachusetts Anti-Slavery Society. Later, he started his own antislavery newspaper, the *North Star*, in 1847.

In 1852, on the day after Independence Day, Douglass gave a speech for the Ladies' Anti-Slavery Society in Rochester, New York. The speech was later called "What to the Slave Is the Fourth of July?" Douglass talked about Americans' most special holiday, and he told it exactly like it was. He started off so nice and meek that he almost seemed to be apologizing for being there, but then, when he got all those white folks all relaxed and comfortable, he sprang this on them:

> Fellow-citizens, pardon me, allow me to ask, why am I called upon to speak here to-day? What have I, or those I represent, to do with your national independence? Are the great principles of political freedom and of natural justice, embodied in that Declaration of Independence, extended to us? . . . I am not included within the pale of this glorious anniversary! Your high independence only reveals the immeasurable distance between us. The blessings in which you, this day, rejoice, are not enjoyed in common. The rich inheritance of justice, liberty, prosperity and independence, bequeathed by your fathers, is

shared by you, not by me. The sunlight that brought life and healing to you, has brought stripes and death to me. This Fourth [of] July is yours, not mine. You may rejoice, I must mourn. To drag a man in fetters into the grand illuminated temple of liberty, and call upon him to join you in joyous anthems, were inhuman mockery and sacrilegious irony. Do you mean, citizens, to mock me, by asking me to speak to-day? If so, there is a parallel to your conduct.

That was Fred. All white folks had to do was teach him to use their language, and he was able to use it a lot better than most of them ever would. After the Civil War started, he helped recruit black soldiers for the Fifty-Fourth Massachusetts Infantry Regiment to fight against the South and slavery. Years later, after the war was over, the president appointed him minister to Haiti. Fred was one black man who believed in himself and his own potential. Not bad for a brotha who started off as somebody else's property, right?

Harriet Tubman

The U.S. Treasury Department has been talking about putting a sister on the twenty-dollar bill: Harriet Tubman. You know if anything like that happens, black folks had nothing to do with it, because if we did, her picture would be lighter and her hair would be straight. Because that's how many of us think. But when you stop and think about Harriet Tubman, and the reason we know about her: white historians picked the woman *they* wanted. You think out of millions of blacks who were slaves, there was only one woman out there helping slaves escape? They picked the one *they* wanted, and then they told us, "Now you leave us alone, okay? See if you can find another one. You ain't got half enough money to do the research, and if you don't do the research, you can't find out." When we stop and think about where we are, we realize we have to challenge everything folks say, even when it sounds good—like putting Harriet Tubman on the twenty-dollar bill.

Now, that's not to take anything away from Harriet Tubman. She was a hero, sure enough. She was a little slip of a woman, wasn't big as a minute, couldn't read or write. All her life, she had dizzy spells because she once got hit in the head with a piece of metal a slave owner had chucked at another slave. That doesn't sound much like somebody who could lead runaway slaves to Canada, does it? But she did, and if you were one of the slaves she was taking and you got scared and wanted to turn back, she'd pull out a pistol and threaten to shoot you. She may have been a little woman, but she was a *serious* little woman.

She was born with the name Araminta Harriet Ross in 1822. She had eight brothers and sisters. Like Frederick Douglass, she was a rebel. One time, she stole some sugar and thought her owner was going to beat her for it, so she hid for five days. She had no love for slavery, and getting hit on the head with that piece of metal didn't help. Things like that—plus seeing family members sold away—made her decide she needed to escape. By then, she had a husband, John Tubman, but when he wouldn't run away with her, and she couldn't get anybody else in her family to go with her, she took off by herself. She made it to New Jersey on foot and became a paid domestic worker. Then she decided she wanted to sneak back down south and free her family, too. She started with her parents, who were old at that point. Before she was done, she had freed many slaves. Nobody knows how many—some say around a hundred fifty, some say three hundred. They called her "Black Moses" because she freed her people like Moses in the Bible freed the Hebrews from Egypt. Except in the case of Moses, we have to take the Bible's word for it. There are *pictures* of Harriet Tubman.

She was a spy, too. During the Civil War, when the white officers needed to know what was going on down south, they'd send free blacks like Harriet, because they could pass as slaves. Nobody'd think twice about seeing one more black person, especially one who looked as little and harmless as Harriet Tubman. We shouldn't be underestimated.

Eli Whitney and the Cotton Gin

Now, they tell you that a white man named Eli Whitney invented the cotton gin in 1793 and put a patent on it the next year. The cotton gin is a machine that separates cotton from cotton seeds. Up until then, black people, slaves, had to do that by hand. The slaves worked themselves to death picking the stuff, but slave owners didn't care, because they didn't care about anything when it came to slaves, as long as those slaves were working. But they say a white man invented the cotton gin, so the job would be easier.

If you never liked me, then why would you invent a cotton gin to ease my burden? The only people who care how hard it is are the people doing it. That's why, when Eli Whitney went to Virginia to visit his mother and father's friend, he saw these slaves sitting out there with this device we now call the cotton gin. And he went back and put a patent on it.

The Dred Scott Decision

Look at what was happening in the first half of the 1800s, the decades before the Civil War. The country didn't know what to do about slavery. The South wanted it, and the North didn't, and the two sides kept coming up with agreements that didn't work out. The Missouri Compromise of 1820 made it so there couldn't be slavery in the Louisiana Territory north of a certain point. Both sides agreed. Then, in 1854, Congress passed the Kansas-Nebraska Act, which let people living in the new territories of Kansas and Nebraska decide for themselves what to do about the issue of slavery. Because Kansas and Nebraska were in the old Louisiana Territory, and because they were north of where the Missouri Compromise said there couldn't be slavery, passing the Kansas-Nebraska Act was about the same as tearing up the Missouri Compromise into little pieces. The proslavery folks were happy. The antislavery folks were angry. And *those* angry folks, the ones who wanted no parts of slavery, were the ones who started the Republican Party.

Then came the Dred Scott decision, in 1857. It was a huge case, man. Dred Scott was a slave in Missouri. His master moved for a while to a spot in the northern part of the Louisiana Territory and took Scott with him. They later went back to Missouri. After that, Scott sued his master. He said that since he had been on soil that was supposed to be free, he was now a free man. The case went all the way to the Supreme Court. The Court pretty much told Dred Scott that negroes were inferior, that they had no rights that the white man was bound to respect.

It seemed that the highest court in the land was on the side of slavery, and that made the antislavery folks mighty depressed. All of them except Frederick Douglass. His view was pretty much: "Look. All this means is if we want to get rid of slavery, we can't do it with little agreements on pieces of paper. Something *big* has got to happen."

He was right. And something big *did* happen—a couple of

things. First was John Brown's 1859 raid on Harpers Ferry, which I'll get to in just a minute. Then, in 1860, the new Republican Party's man, Abraham Lincoln, got elected. In 1863, Lincoln freed the slaves—on paper, anyway—with the Emancipation Proclamation.

As bad as the Dred Scott decision was, it helped folks see what needed to happen.

John Brown and the Outbreak of the Civil War

There wouldn't have been a Civil War without John Brown.

People will say, "Oh, John Brown was crazy." You ask them, "Why you say that?" and they'll say, "Well, look at what he did in Kansas." What did he do in Kansas? "He killed people in Kansas."

Yeah, but do they know *why* he did it?

Today, when they have presidential elections, people talk about "battleground states." Man, let me tell you, most folks today don't know what a battleground state is all *about*. As I mentioned earlier, in 1854 the U.S. government passed the Kansas-Nebraska Act. That meant that some land they stole from Native Americans would be the U.S. territories that became the states of Kansas and Nebraska. It also meant that the people who lived there could decide whether the states would be free or slave states. Folks from both sides moved to Kansas, ready to fight. I don't mean argue. I mean they got ready to shoot and cut one another to death, and that's what some of them ended up doing. Now *that's* a battleground state.

Well, one of the people who went there was John Brown. After some dirty proslavery dogs raided Lawrence, Kansas, and tore up the offices of some abolitionist newspapers and went crazy looting the rest of the town, John Brown and his men came in and killed five proslavery men—hacked them to death. That same year, 1856, Brown and his men, including his sons, fought against the proslavery forces at the Battle of Black Jack and the Battle of Osawatomie. That was John Brown. I'm not talking about some poor chump who joins the army just so he can make a living and then goes out to kill whomever the government tells him to kill. I'm talking about a man who had a belief so strong that he was willing to die for it.

I've said it once before: white is not a color; it's an attitude. By skin color, John Brown was a white man, but he may have been the best friend black folks ever had. He believed that slavery was straight up evil, and he didn't want to hear about peaceful opposition to slavery—he knew it would take *action* to get rid of that mess. In 1859, when he decided to raid Harpers Ferry, in Virginia (now in West Virginia), he had twenty-one people with him, five of them black. Now, Harpers Ferry was the U.S. government munitions place, where weapons were made, so it was full of military rifles and bullets. The government had four divisions of troops guarding it. Brown and fewer than two dozen men got in there, killed four people, wounded a bunch more, and held the soldiers off for two days—*two days* before the soldiers could break in the engine room where John Brown and his men were holed up.

Now, there's a reason I would place John Brown as one of the most important people who ever lived in the history of planet Earth. Here is a man who not only decided to kill for me and die for me, but he took his own sons with him. You can't risk more than that; you can't sacrifice more than that. Even now, I go to the site every year on my birthday, and then I go back on October 16. That's the day of the raid. And then I go on December 2, which is the day they hanged him. You think Lincoln didn't know what he was doing when he put that statue of freedom at the US Capitol facing east? He put that there on December 2, 1863. He didn't say it was in honor of John Brown, but think about it.

When John Brown was about to die, somebody yelled up at him, "How you feel now, nigger lover?" He said, "What I'm dying for, if I was defending rich white men, I'd be your hero." And when he hit the last step up to the gallows and the noose they were going to hang him with, he said, "*Oh*, by the way, I talked to God last night and God told me to tell you that you missed the last chance of freeing the Negro without bloodshed." Brown continued: the Negro would be freed, and it would be the biggest bloodbath in the history of war.

The American Civil War was the first war in history where soldiers on both sides had gone to the same school, West Point. They knew each other's strategies. That's why the war dragged on like that. There hadn't ever been a war like that. That was some nasty stuff. The two sides would stand there and shoot at each other, and when they ran out of bullets, then the *real* thing started: charging at each other and scooping out each other's guts with those bayonets, until the ground and everybody on it was covered in red. If there's a hell, it must look a lot like that.

It was because of John Brown. They killed John Brown, and eighteen months later, the war started, because after what Brown and his men did, there was no turning back. Slavery was going to end or it was going to continue, but either way, the question of slavery was going to be decided through bloodshed. And during the war, what were the Northern soldiers singing? "John Brown's body lies a-moulderin' in the grave." Not "God Bless America," but "John Brown's Body."

You see, racist whites weren't satisfied with just killing John Brown. After he was dead, they sent word: "We're not going to let John Brown's body get back to New York." When black men heard that, we lined the roads from Harpers Ferry to that little town in New York where Brown was buried—*lined the roads*, shoulder to shoulder, saying, "Come on, y'all. Come on, just try to get him." And that's how Brown's body got back home: black men saying, "You think you gonna stop something? You will over our dead bodies."

The Fifty-Fourth Massachusetts Infantry Regiment

Next time you hear some racist say, "Black people don't want to do anything to help themselves," tell him about the black soldiers who enlisted in the Union Army during the Civil War. See what he has to say then.

Truth is, 186,000 black soldiers enlisted. Around 50,000 came from free states, and another 40,000 came from what they called border states—those were slaves states that hadn't seceded from the Union. In those states, some fought for the Union, some for the Confederacy. But the biggest number of black soldiers, about 93,000, came from the Southern states that *had* left the Union. All of them were called the "United States Colored Troops."

Mostly they were led by white officers. The white officers weren't exactly fighting each other over the chance to command the blacks. That changed, though, after the blacks proved they could fight well and bravely and after their regiments started to make a name for themselves. It was no different with the black soldiers. Four men from the all-black Fifty-Fourth Massachusetts Infantry—that's the regiment whose story is told in *Glory*—won medals for gallantry after their assault on Fort Wagner, on Morris Island, South Carolina, in July 1863. They were gallant, all right. A whole bunch of them gave up their lives.

Just like with everything else black folks tried to do in those days, the first thing black soldiers had to do was convince white folks that we were up to the job. At first the Union didn't want black soldiers. When the Civil War was heading into its third year and the South was showing no signs of giving up, getting help from black soldiers finally started to seem like a good idea. After Abraham Lincoln signed the Emancipation Proclamation, freeing the slaves, a black leader in Boston named Lewis Hayden convinced the abolitionist governor of Massachusetts, John Andrew, to put together a regiment of black soldiers. That's how the Fifty-Fourth was born.

A Union general, Quincy Gillmore, wanted to capture South Carolina, which a lot of folks thought of as the heart of the Confederacy. To do that, they had to get past a few strongholds, and one of the strongest was Fort Wagner. Trying to take out Wagner was like trying to knock somebody out in a boxing ring—that is, if the ring were hip-deep in water and sand and your opponent were wearing body armor. Wagner was on a strip of land with the Atlantic on one side and a swamp on the other. The fort was thirty feet high, two hundred fifty by one hundred yards in size, and made of sand. That might not sound very strong, but it was fortified with logs and sandbags, and it had wooden spikes in front of it, spikes sharp enough to go right through you, plus land mines—step on one of those and it'd be the last step you ever took in this life. Wagner had a moat around it, too. And did I mention the fourteen cannons sticking out of it? I give those Southern folks this much: they knew how to play defense.

The Union wasn't stupid. They knew if they just charged Fort Wagner they'd get shot down like ducks. So, before they did, they tried firing shells at it. Problem was, Wagner had what they called a "bombproof": roof beams with ten feet of sand on top of them. The Fifty-Fourth spent most of the day shooting shells at that thing, and after about eleven hours it was still standing. Still, the Union figured they had softened it up enough so the soldiers could take it.

That's where the Fifty-Fourth came in. One of them was Lewis Henry Douglass, Frederick Douglass's son. They were commanded by Col. Robert Gould Shaw—skinny white dude, wasn't but twenty-five years old. His parents were abolitionists. At that point, Colonel Shaw ordered 624 men from the Fifty-Fourth to quick-march in with muskets and bayonets. As they got closer to Fort Wagner, they started to jog. When they were close enough, the Confederates inside the fort fired on them. Some from the Fifty-Fourth fell, but the others kept going. The wooden spikes didn't stop them—they climbed right over that crap. The moat didn't stop them, either—all the shelling had half-filled it with sand. But the Confederates didn't stop firing, either. The Fifty-Fourth got mowed down. Colonel Shaw got killed, too, as did the waves of soldiers the Union sent in after the Fifty-Fourth. When it was all over, the fort still hadn't fallen.

The Fifty-Fourth didn't succeed that day. But they were as brave as all hell, and they were fighting for black folks' freedom—and for the country, to keep it in one piece, North and South. They made the biggest sacrifice you can make.

Jocko

The way something *looks* is not always the way it *is*, and what white folks say is *definitely* not always the truth. Do I really have to remind you of that?

For instance, when I was a boy, a friend of mine and I used to go out in the suburbs and throw bricks at those little black jockeys—you know, the ones you see holding lanterns on white folks' lawns.

Then, one day I said, "Hey, man. Something's not right about this. Jockeys don't carry lanterns." We decided to see what was up.

We got to looking and looking and looking, and then I found out that the "jockey" who started it all, the one behind those statues, wasn't a jockey at all. He was a twelve-year-old boy and—are you ready?—General George Washington's number one war strategist. Name was Jocko Graves. He was the son of Tom Graves, a free black man in Washington's army. Jocko wanted to fight in the army, too, but he was too young. That didn't stop him from traveling with Washington and the troops. That little black boy wanted to go, so he *went*. Simple as that.

One morning, Jocko saw General Washington, and it looked like something was bothering him, so Jocko said, "What's wrong, Pop?"

Washington said, "Ah, nothing."

Jocko said, "Come on. You worried 'bout something."

Washington told him, "We think the British are going to come in at this point, down *here*, and we'll be waiting for them. But there's also a possibility they'll come in over *there*. I can't divide my troops." That little twelve-year-old said, "Don't worry. I think you're right, but give me that lantern. If they come that way, I can see them if they come around that bend."

It turned out George Washington was right. His army battled the British all night, killed them all. When Washington ran over to where Jocko was holding that lantern to keep a lookout for the British, he saw that the boy had frozen to death. Now *that's* loyalty.

That's why I say you can't trust what folks tell you. They reduced that story down to just some little tar-black jockey-looking kid holding a lantern on white folks' lawns, when the real story is about loyalty. Twelve-year-old black boy froze to death protecting the American revolutionaries.

Even the white folks who know the story tell it wrong. According to them, Jocko froze to death holding the reins of Washington's horses—this shows Jocko's loyalty, but holding reins didn't require brains. Don't pay attention to that mess.

The Assassination of Abraham Lincoln

People talk about Abraham Lincoln like he was the best friend black folks ever had because he freed the slaves. Lincoln didn't care a thing about black folks, and he sure wasn't their best friend. Now, you can look this up: Lincoln met with a roomful of black men in the White House and told them they weren't as smart as white folks. One of his ideas for what to do after slavery was round up black folks and send them to another country. Think about your best friend. Would he or she tell you to your face you're as stupid as the day is long, and then try to get you to move out of the country? If the answer is yes, you need a new best friend. Or else, maybe your friend is right about the stupid part.

Lincoln didn't care one way or another about black folks, or about slavery, either. He wanted to preserve the Union, that's all. Here's what he said: "If I could save the Union without freeing any slave, I would do it. And if I could save it by freeing all the slaves, I would do it. And if I could save it by freeing some, and leaving others alone, I would do that." Now, maybe that doesn't sound like somebody who hates black people. It doesn't exactly sound like somebody with their best interests at heart, either, does it? Abraham Lincoln was a white man of his time. That's the long and the short of it.

Folks say Lincoln got killed for freeing black folks. Maybe. Maybe not.

Think about this a minute. Lincoln was president during the

Civil War, after the Southern states had seceded from the United States, and he had to find a way to preserve that Union he cared so much about. (You know, the one blacks built for free during slavery.) Now, it takes money to fight a war. If you're fighting in the army but you don't get paid, pretty soon you might just stop fighting. Plus, you've got to *eat*. The government has to pay for all that. Well, the government didn't have enough money. So, Lincoln went to banks in New York and asked to borrow what he needed. The banks said, "Sure. But you have to pay us back at 36 percent interest." That meant the U.S. government would have to pay the banks back every dime it borrowed plus another one-third on top of that. That's like if you ask your neighbor to borrow his screwdriver and he says, "Sure, you can borrow it, but when you bring it back, you've got to give me some screws along with it." Lincoln said, "Later for that."

What did Lincoln do instead? He ordered the government to print money. Called it "greenbacks." Before that point in U.S. history, anytime the government printed a dollar, it had to have a dollar's worth of gold to back it up. But with the North fighting a war and Lincoln needing a way to pay for it, in 1862 Lincoln said, "Go ahead and print money." That way, the thinking went, the government wouldn't owe money to the banks. All this new money was floating around, and the banks didn't have a thing to do with it. If you think the banks liked that, think again.

Now, go forward almost exactly a hundred years, when we had another president who was supposed to be a friend to black folks: John F. Kennedy. Comes into office, starts making all kind of noise about what he's going to do for blacks. Of course, he didn't get a chance to do it—if that's what he was really going to do—because in Dallas, Texas, on November 22, 1963, he was assassinated. All his plans fell to his vice president, Lyndon B. Johnson.

People like to say Kennedy was killed for what he wanted to do for black folks. Maybe, maybe not.

Look here: On June 4, 1963, Kennedy signed Executive Order No. 11110, which allowed the U.S. government, once again, to print money without going through the Federal Reserve Bank. In other words, the government could get money without owing one thin dime to the bankers. So, once again, there was new money but no action for the banks. The whole reason the Federal Reserve Bank exists is to lend money to the government and get paid back with interest. If it can't do that, it's out of business. If you think the Federal Reserve bankers wanted that, think again. Kennedy got killed five months later. Folks said it was because he supported civil rights, but he was also one of two presidents who tried to get around the banks. The other one was Abraham Lincoln.

What do *you* think?

2

Solidarity

Free people are the ones with enough money to control the information the rest of us get.

We can't believe in others, we have to believe in black solidarity. The point is we can have help from white folks but we can't rely on them. We have to organize ourselves. We've done so in the past and we need to do it some more. In this section I highlight ways in which Blacks have organized and produced great outcomes.

W. E. B. Du Bois, Booker T. Washington, and the Atlanta Compromise

Here's something that might seem strange. At the same time that some white folks were making things tough for black people in the South, other white folks couldn't throw money at blacks fast enough. Most of the money had to do with education. Some of the rich folks giving out all the money, the philanthropists, did it partly out of the goodness of their hearts. Some of them were church folks and were just trying to do their Christian duty. But some of them, especially the ones in the North, figured it this way: if folks in the South (including black folks) got enough education to get good jobs, they could pay their fair share of taxes. See there? With half of what goes on in life, if you dig down to the bottom to see what it's all about, you find money. (With the other half, you find sex. But that's a different story.)

Here's how strange it was. After slavery came a dozen years of Reconstruction, and it seemed like a new day for black folks in the South. Because there were federal troops ensuring our rights, blacks could vote and run for office with little trouble, and there were even black senators and congressmen down South. Then came the presidential election of 1876. It was a close one. It looked like the Democrat, Samuel Tilden, had more votes in the Electoral College than the Republican, Rutherford B. Hayes. Some said otherwise, because the vote in a few states was so close that nobody knew whom the states' electoral votes were going to. (There wasn't a presidential election like that again until 124 years later, when George W. Bush ran against Al Gore in 2000.) Finally, the Democrats said, "Okay, look here. Y'all can have the election. No problem. You just have to do us one favor. Take these federal troops out of the South—you know, the ones y'all got down here making sure blacks can vote and get elected to office. Let us deal with our black people *our* way." The Republicans said, "Cool," and that's how the Compromise of 1877 happened. Hayes became president, and just about the first thing he did was remove the troops from the South. And just like that, Reconstruction was over.

Now, here's the strange part. Rutherford B. Hayes, the man who became president on the condition that he pull federal troops out of the South and end Reconstruction—*that same man* later helped run a fund that helped a dozen schools train black teachers. Isn't that some crazy stuff?

Even after the government pulled the federal troops out of the South, and even after blacks got chased out of Congress with white dudes in hoods two steps behind them, and even when some blacks were getting locked up just for looking white folks in the eye—while all that was happening, black folks were going to *school*. If they couldn't do anything else for them, poor black parents were at least able to send their kids to school.

One of those little kids was young Booker T. Washington. He was born in Virginia in 1856 as a slave. Then, after Emancipation, he went to school at the Hampton Institute, in Virginia. That school was run by Gen. Samuel Chapman Armstrong. And that's who gave old Booker T. the main idea he didn't let go of for the rest of his life: it was all about *work*. If you were working, you were staying out of trouble. The more work you did, the better you got at it, and the better you got, the more money you made, and the prouder you felt. The prouder you felt, the more you stayed out of trouble, because you didn't want to mess it all up doing some low-down mess. The more money you made, the more property you would have, and the more property you had, the more you would have to keep and protect—so the harder you'd work. For Booker T., it all started and ended with work. Booker T. Washington believed that for black folks in the South, which is where most of them were at the time, the key was to find work that white folks needed done. That way, black folks would be useful to other people, and when other people needed you, you survived. Not just that: if black folks showed white folks we could work and be trusted, if we proved that our presence was good for white people, the whites might just let up on us and treat us like ordinary folks instead of animals. What kind of work did white folks need done? Farming and other manual labor. Stuff like that. See, Booker T. was all for blacks getting educated, as long as we got taught to do *practical* stuff.

General Armstrong recommended Booker T. to head up the Tuskegee Institute, a school in Alabama for black folks that got started in the 1880s. Booker ran Tuskegee for the rest of his life. It gave his ideas a spotlight. He thought the most important thing was for blacks to get themselves together economically. Racial equality? Fighting for voting rights? Integrating with whites? The way Booker T. saw it, all that could wait. It was more important to *work*.

You'd best believe white people ate that stuff up. Why wouldn't they have? They didn't have to change a thing they were doing, and black folks were going to help them.

In 1895 in Georgia, Booker T. gave a famous talk that was known afterward as the Atlanta Compromise speech. He said about blacks and whites, "In all things that are purely social we can be as separate as the five fingers, yet one as the hand in all things essential to mutual progress." White people clapped at that till they couldn't feel their hands! Washington told blacks in the South that they should forget about going somewhere else to make a new start. They had opportunities right where they were. He said, "To those of my race who depend upon bettering their condition in a foreign land or who underestimate the importance of cultivating friendly relations with the Southern white man . . . I would say 'Cast down your bucket where you are'—cast it down in making friends in every manly way of the people of all races by whom we are surrounded. Cast it down in agriculture, mechanics, in commerce, in domestic service, and in the professions."

Of course, now it probably won't surprise you to hear that not all black people saw things the way he did. Some black folks heard what Booker T. was saying about doing what white folks needed done, and they said, "Later for that. The Fourteenth Amendment says I'm a citizen. If I'm a citizen, I've got rights, and I should be able to do what I want. Forget about trying to do what the white folks need. That mess ended with slavery, or should have. Why have I got to try to be useful to the white man just so he won't treat me worse than he treats a dog? I've got my own life to think about. I need to be able to vote. That's my right as a citizen. If I want to spend my life studying philosophy or French or art history, I need to be able to do *that*. What I want doesn't have a thing to do with the white man."

One brother who felt that way was William Edward Burghardt Du Bois—W.E.B. for short. He was born in Massachusetts in 1868. Talk about a black man getting educated: after he got a degree at Fisk University, Du Bois went overseas to study in Berlin, then returned and became the first black person to get a PhD from Harvard University. That man had brains coming out of his *ears*. (One of Du Bois's books is *The Souls of Black Folk*, which you need to read, if you haven't.) Du Bois didn't like what Booker T. Washington was saying, and not just because he thought black people should be able to do whatever we wanted. The way Du Bois saw it, if all you told black people to do was work, work, and work some more, you were making them into machines instead of people. In an essay called "The Talented Tenth," Du Bois wrote, "If we make money the object of man-training, we shall develop money-makers but not necessarily men; if we make technical skill the object of education, we may possess artisans but not, in nature, men. Men we shall have only as we make manhood the object of the work of the schools—intelligence, broad sympathy, knowledge of the world that was and is, and of the relation of men to it—this is the curriculum of that Higher Education which must underlie true life."

The Founding of the NAACP

In the nineteenth century, black folks couldn't win for losing. Things looked good for a while. In 1863, President Abraham Lincoln announced the end of slavery with the Emancipation Proclamation, and the slaveholding states that made up the Confederacy lost the war in 1865. It was a new day for black folks—or at least it seemed that way. Reconstruction started but was short-lived. Black folks didn't go back to being slaves, and we still had the *legal* right to vote, because of the Fifteenth Amendment, which got passed in 1870. But that didn't stop southerners from harassing blacks at the polls and making us take all kinds of stupid tests before we could get anywhere near a ballot box. So, black people could vote but we couldn't vote.

Now, it wasn't enough for some white folks that blacks were prevented from voting or serving in office. Because black people weren't slaves anymore, we were getting jobs that whites felt entitled to. Whites didn't like that a bit. Plus, how could white folks feel they were better than blacks if blacks were free just like them? Some black people had even been congressmen and senators. A lot of white folks didn't like that, either. They started getting resentful—as if they were the ones who had something to be resentful about! They got so pissed off at black people that they started lynching us. Between the mid-1880s and 1900, more than 2,500 folks were lynched. Most of these were black folks, and most of the lynchings were in the southern states—and those are just the ones we know about, after they finally started keeping track!

It wasn't just lynchings, either. Sometimes whole black neighborhoods got burned down. If word got out that some black person had done some white person wrong—even if it hadn't happened—the next thing you knew, there was a white mob beating and killing the accused black person, torching his house. It didn't happen just in the South, either. In Springfield, Illinois, in 1908, a couple of black men accused of rape and murder (which they hadn't committed) were transferred from one prison to another before a mob could lynch them. That upset the mob so bad they burned up $200,000 worth of black folks' property.

That was the racial climate at the time the National Association for the Advancement of Colored People, or the NAACP, got started. Folks today talk about "climate change." Some climates change, some don't.

In 1909, the year after the Springfield riot, a group of black *and* white folks decided that enough was enough. Matter of fact, the white folks were the ones who called the first meeting. Only a handful of black folks were involved at the beginning, including Mary Church Terrell, Ida B. Wells, and W. E. B. Du Bois.

Still, it wasn't as if black folks hadn't been active in our own defense up till that point. In 1905, Du Bois and another black man, William Monroe Trotter, had started the Niagara Movement to oppose discrimination and fight for black people's rights. But half the fighting the group did was with one another—they couldn't agree on which candidate to support for president or on other issues. Things got so bad that Trotter left the group in 1907, and by the time the NAACP formed, Du Bois told the handful of members left in the Niagara Movement to throw their support behind the NAACP. Du Bois headed up the NAACP's magazine, *The Crisis*, which is still being published today.

Now, hard as they tried, the NAACP couldn't get Congress to pass anti-lynching laws. There were too many racist congressmen and senators for that, and even if they weren't racist themselves, some of the voters in their districts were, and those voters had long memories. The NAACP did publish a report, *Thirty Years of Lynching in the United States, 1889–1919*, that became the talk of the land and helped lead to a decline in the number of lynchings.

The NAACP had its national office in New York City, and field offices in Boston, Washington, Detroit, and other cities, and then it spread out even more. In the 1930s, when the Depression hit and the whole country was suffering—and blacks were suffering worse—the NAACP fought to get black folks jobs.

The NAACP was also behind the cases that got combined in *Brown v. Board of Education of Topeka, Kansas*, in 1954, which was when the U.S. Supreme Court decided that school segregation and the Constitution didn't see eye to eye. Since then, the NAACP has been involved in activities ranging from the civil rights movement to the fight to get more black characters on TV shows like *The West Wing*.

The Great Migration and the Urban League

In the nineteenth century, most black folks in America lived in the South. Early in the twentieth century, we started moving north and west. A whole lot of things made us move.

Here's one: right after the Civil War ended, the southern states, starting with South Carolina and Mississippi, passed the Black Codes. Among other things, that meant if you were black and got called a vagrant, you would get arrested. It was pretty easy to get called a vagrant. Black people had to have written proof of employment on us at all times, and if we didn't, we could get arrested. We had to sign work contracts, and if we tried to get out of those contracts before the end of the year, we had to pay back the year's wages or get arrested. And not only did we have to work and prove we were working, but there were only a couple of kinds of work we could *do*. In South Carolina, if you were black and wanted a job as anything besides a farmer or a servant, you had to pay a tax, which most black folks couldn't afford. That way, white folks had guaranteed labor. Besides, who did you think you were, trying to be something besides a servant, you uppity nigger, you?

What happened when black people got arrested? That's the beautiful part. We still had to work, but now we had to do it for *free* again. Just like in slavery times. It was called convict leasing. Prisons would "lease" convicts out to companies for mining work and other dangerous, dirty jobs, and the convicts didn't get paid a cent. The only difference between that and slavery is this: If a slave master owned you, he didn't want you to die, because he'd paid money for you. But if you were a prisoner and got worked to death, there were plenty more where you came from.

And when racist whites weren't trapping you, tricking you, and arresting you, they were up and killing you.

So, if you were black and living in the South, and all that mess was going on, the North and West would've started looking pretty good, right?

The only problem (*besides* having to leave behind your home and everything you ever knew) was the white bosses didn't want to let you go. They had other plans for you. (It's nice to feel wanted, but not like *that*.) So, you couldn't just walk into work one day and tell your boss, "I quits! Going up north! Good-bye, you old racist dog, you!" If you tried to do that, the boss would find a way to put you in jail, or kill you. No, you had to get slick about it. Pretend you were just going out for a drive, then hop on that train and not look back.

So, now you're up north or out west, along with the more than half a million other black folks who between 1910 and 1920 alone had enough sense and balls to hightail it out of the South. Things are better where you've gone to, but it's not like New York City, Chicago, Philadelphia, or Los Angeles held a ticker-tape parade for you and put up banners reading, "Welcome, Negro Friends!" Black folks still had to face the big three: segregation, discrimination, and poverty. In the only parts of town black folks could go to, we got charged too much money for places that were falling apart because landlords knew we couldn't go anywhere else. Racism in housing, racism in employment, racism in education—it was all there waiting for us.

Just like with the NAACP, black *and* white folks got together and decided that that crap wasn't acceptable. For a while, it seemed that for every black person who had come north, there was a group trying to help him out! The Committee on Urban Conditions Among Negroes got started in 1910 in New York. Of course, we already had the Committee for the Improvement of Industrial Conditions Among Negroes in New York, which had come along in 1906. And did I mention that the National League for the Protection of Colored Women had been founded in 1905? Eventually they all merged, but the new name, the National League on Urban Conditions Among Negroes, wasn't too much better, so, in 1920, they shortened it to the National Urban League. That was more like it. And that group has been around ever since, helping black folks fight discrimination in education, jobs, housing, and health care.

Congress of Racial Equality (CORE)

Now, you can't really understand Martin Luther King Jr. until you know a little something about Mahatma Gandhi. Gandhi was Indian. For a bald little man with no teeth, he was a mighty strong dude, leading the Indian people to their independence from Britain, which they finally got in 1947. He did it through what he called "noncooperation" and passive resistance. Gandhi didn't want violence. His whole thing was this: Britain couldn't keep on ruling India without Indians' cooperation, so what Indians had to do was just stop cooperating. It was simple and beautiful: don't hit anybody, but *just don't do what they tell you to do.* And the plan *worked.* Indians stopped buying the stuff Britain made, stopped going to school, stopped going to work, and went to jail until the jails couldn't hold one more Indian. Finally, the British said, "All right, enough, you win."

A lot of people know that Gandhi influenced Martin Luther King Jr.'s philosophy of nonviolent resistance in the civil rights movement. What a lot of people don't know is how many *others* Gandhi influenced. One group that admired his teachings was the Congress of Racial Equality, which got started in Chicago in 1942.

Called the Committee of Racial Equality at first, CORE was an integrated group. One of the original members was a black man, James Farmer. The group came out of another organization, the Fellowship of Reconciliation. Like Gandhi, the group was dedicated to nonviolent action. It succeeded in integrating public places in the North through sit-ins like the ones that would become famous in the South.

At first, CORE wasn't merely pacifist, or nonviolent. Its members didn't believe in hierarchies, either. In other words, nobody was really in charge. That became a problem when the group started to expand nationwide. Ever been to a meeting where nobody is in charge? It's cool and everything—until you try to get something done. Then you realize you've got a problem. Finally, the national organization took a firm hand and told the local chapters to fall in line. James Farmer became president in 1953.

Things heated up when the group started being active in the South. In 1960, the U.S. Supreme Court had declared that segregation in interstate bus travel was unconstitutional. CORE decided to test out if that ruling was being enforced, sending groups of blacks and whites together on buses headed south. Those were some brave folks. They were beaten by mobs, and the buses were set on fire—and the only thing the local police did was throw some of the *riders* in jail. Still, the Freedom Rides—that's what we called them—went on. And they worked. In fact, there was such an uproar over the Freedom Riders' treatment in the South that the Interstate Commerce Commission finally ended segregation of buses and travel facilities, including restrooms.

CORE was involved in voter registration drives in the South, too. Three of the CORE workers in Mississippi during the Freedom Summer, 1964, were James Chaney, a young black man, and two young white dudes, Andrew Goodman and Michael Schwerner. For their trouble, they were beaten and murdered by the Ku Klux Klan, with the cooperation of the local police.

Art Stoyer was a brilliant human being, writer, and researcher, and one of my best friends. He was white. That's how you know that there are a whole lot of people out here willing to die for what's right. One day before the murders of Chaney, Goodman, and Schwerner, Art and I left for Russia to protest the death of an African man who had been murdered, frozen to death, because he was dating a white woman. When we arrived, we had planned to march the following day around Red Square to let the world know that racism exists in Russia and affects many victims (not just black folks). Similar to America, where racism/white supremacy didn't stop with black folks but included Native Americans, Latinos, Asians, Jews, Irish Catholics, and many others, not to mention women. So we had a guy in Russia make us some signs that night. That morning Art and I woke up planning to picket but we found out to our horror that three CORE members had been murdered. James Chaney, a black man, and two white Jewish men named Andrew Goodman and Michael Schwerner had been murdered by the Ku Klux Klan with the aid of law enforcement. We canceled our demonstration in Russia and caught a plane back to America and went to Philadelphia, Mississippi. I called Hugh Hefner and asked him if he'd send my wife $25,000 cash, and said I would give it back to him when I came home from Mississippi. After Lil put the money in the bank, I announced that I was putting $25,000 up for a reward for the arrest and conviction of the murderers. We left that morning on the first plane and by that evening (because of the time difference) were looking the sheriff in the eye, telling him, "We know you did this, with the help of others!" Unbeknownst to Art and me, the FBI had never put up a reward in their history. So hearing that we had put up $25,000, the FBI decided to put up a $30,000 reward. That's the only decent thing that the FBI did, even though they did it for reasons that had nothing to do with decency. The guy who got in touch with the FBI and me told us both that he knew who did it. (He wanted to collect the $25,000 from me and the $30,000 from the FBI.) For months they looked for the bodies of these three young CORE workers with no luck. Finally, I held a press conference in San Francisco and said if the bodies aren't found by twelve noon tomorrow, I will change my schedule and go back to Mississippi and get some CORE workers, get some shovels, and go under the bridge where the bodies were. Needless to say, the federal authorities dug up the bodies before twelve noon. This was all thanks to the guy who was trying hustle the FBI and Dick Gregory for the money. The authorities knew there were twenty some odd people involved. Of all the people they arrested, two were not involved at all. Therefore they couldn't get a conviction for any of them because the two that weren't involved were able to prove that they were in jail during the murders. That's how the government works.

So, the next time it's Election Day and you're too tired to make it to the voting booth, or you've got other plans, or you just don't feel like it, or you have some other lame excuse, think about the folks who got beaten and risked death and gave up their lives so people who looked like you could cast a ballot. It doesn't mean you have to support "the lesser of two evils." You keep doing that and you start to feel a little bit evil your own self. But whatever you do, get out there and *vote*, man.

Adam Clayton Powell Jr.

When Adam Clayton Powell Jr. was in Congress, from 1945 to 1971, he wrote something like 98 percent of the social legislation on this planet, and he inspired a lot of other lawmakers who came after him. Brilliant! God, was he brilliant!

Brother Adam was—you know how there are some people you'd like to see one more time on this earth? Well, for me, one of them is Adam. He went to Colgate University; the average white person around him didn't know what Colgate was. They thought it was a kind of toothpaste. But he carried himself like he didn't have to apologize for anything. At the time, he was one of the greatest preachers in America (if not *the* greatest), and there was nobody in Hollywood as handsome as he was.

His colleagues were a pool of white men who wrote legislation that affected the whole world. Adam had the same position they did, but that didn't stop him from coming up against racism. Take, for instance, the story of when he went to the Congressional Dining Hall one day. A sergeant at arms said to him, "Where you going, nigger?"

Adam said, "You talking to me?"

"Yeah, nigger."

"Um, I'm going to eat."

"Niggers can't eat here."

"Well, where do we—?"

"There's a place about ten miles from here where all the educated, sophisticated niggers go."

"So how do I get there?"

"Well, you can take a cab. The man to see, his name is Billy Simpson."

So, about an hour later, Adam came back to the dining hall with the most ghetto-looking black man you ever saw in your life—scraggly beard, overalls, no shirt, barefoot.

So, the sergeant at arms came up to Adam again and said, "Did you find it, boy?" Then he saw the man Adam had with him and said, "Who is *this*?"

"Oh," Adam said, "this man's name is Billy Simpson. I thought this was who you were telling me about—that the only way I could get in here was to bring this nigger with me." I guess the sergeant didn't know there was more than one Billy Simpson. And that's when all hell broke loose. Adam told the sergeant at arms, "I either come in here or I'm whupping yo behind and I'm throwing all the food away." That was Adam.

Adam was born in Connecticut in 1908. His parents were of mixed race. The same year he was born, his father became pastor of the Abyssinian Baptist Church in Harlem, which had a congregation of ten thousand folks. So, Adam grew up wealthy; he was also light-skinned enough to pass for white, which he did for a while in college.

But he didn't keep that up. He came back to New York City from Colgate, got a master's degree in religious education from Columbia University, and started working in his dad's church. He also became an activist on behalf of black people.

When businesses wouldn't hire black folks, Adam organized pickets and marches. He set up soup kitchens and other services for people in the community, and to draw attention to it all, he founded a newspaper, the *People's Voice*. That helped him win a seat on the New York City Council in 1941.

He ran for Congress in 1944, calling for civil rights and an end to job discrimination against blacks. For the first ten years, he was one of only two blacks in all of Congress. He butted heads with racist southern Democrats. He was outspoken. He made himself heard. He advised presidents to support African countries struggling to win independence, and he was relentless with his civil rights work.

In 1954, the Supreme Court decided, in the matter of *Brown v. Board of Education of Topeka, Kansas*, that segregated schools were unconstitutional, but that didn't mean school districts were in a rush to desegregate. Adam knew that. He wrote up what's called a rider, saying that schools in the South couldn't get federal funds until they fell in line with desegregation, and he attached that rider to a bunch of bills in Congress. That later became part of the Civil Rights Act of 1964. Title VI of the act says there can't be race discrimination in programs that get federal money. We owe that to Adam Clayton Powell Jr.

That's the kind of thing that outraged other congressmen. They were out to get Adam. I don't want to say he was perfect, but neither were his colleagues, and they punished him for doing exactly what they were doing, because he was black and proud and didn't apologize for it. They nailed him for taking trips at public expense and missing committee meetings, taking away his committee chairmanship and finally kicking him out of Congress altogether. Then he won a special election to fill his own vacant seat! He served until 1970, when Charles Rangel beat him in the election.

When his enemies in Congress were coming after him, Adam

said, "I wish to state very emphatically . . . that I will always do just what every other Congressman and committee chairman has done and is doing and will do." That was Adam, a tough, bad black man till the end.

The Murder of Emmett Till

Now, they say Rosa Parks was the spark of the civil rights movement. But I'll tell you who sparked Rosa Parks: Emmett Till's mama, Mamie.

Emmett Till was a fourteen-year-old black boy from Chicago who went to see some relatives in a little town in Mississippi in 1955. The name of the town was Money. Now, isn't that something? It's as if folks wanted to name the town after the thing they cared about the most, but they couldn't call the town "Killing Negroes," so they had to settle for the next best thing.

One day, Emmett was in a store in the town and they said that he looked at and whistled at a twenty-one-year-old white woman, *or so they said*. They called it "reckless eyeballing." Boy, what did he do that for? Couple of days later, the woman's husband and the husband's half-brother went to where Emmett was staying and kidnapped him. What they did to that poor boy—it'd be quicker to tell you what they *didn't* do. When they ran out of ways to torture him, they shot him and threw his body in the Tallahatchie River.

After Emmett's body was pulled from the river and sent back to Chicago for the funeral, that was when Mamie Till gave the world the shock it needed. She insisted on having an open-casket funeral service, so the world could see what those men had done to her boy—the men who got away with it and then later *admitted they'd done it.* So many thousands of people attended that funeral and saw Emmett's body. A whole bunch fainted, and a whole bunch more needed smelling salts. And with good reason—ever seen a monster movie or a zombie movie? I'm telling you, the Oscar-winningest makeup man in Hollywood couldn't make somebody look like that boy looked in his casket. Then John H. Johnson published photos of Emmett's face in *Jet* magazine, and then *everybody* saw it.

Including Rosa Parks.

Carolyn Bryant, Emmett's accuser, recently came forward in 2017 and, in an interview with Timothy Tyson, the author of a new book titled, *The Blood of Emmett Till*, said that she lied about the encounter. She was even quoted saying, "Nothing that boy did could ever justify what happened to him."

Rosa Parks

One day I was talking to Rosa Parks. I said to her, just teasing her, "When you refused to give up your seat on that bus, you wasn't just tired like white folks said you was."

She started crying, and I couldn't believe the answer she gave me.

Martin Luther King Jr., who gets all the credit for everything, was just an earnest Baptist preacher. His consciousness came from the white schools he went to. And he had that twang that Baptist preachers have that white folks can't understand. That's why all we ever heard of him on the TV networks were sound bites—"Goin' to the mountaintop" and the rest of that stuff you hear year in and year out on his birthday.

But think about Rosa Parks and the effect she had on the whole planet. She didn't have a church behind her, like King did, but look what she did. When she refused to give up her bus seat to a white dude, and got arrested for it, black *and* white folks rallied around her.

That day I spoke to her—we were just kicking back, having dinner at a hotel—I was only playing when I said, "Look at your pretty feet. And they wanted to say you wouldn't give up your seat because you were *tired*."

Think about it. White folks try to say that if Rosa hadn't been too tired to get up from her seat that day, none of it would ever have happened—everything that sparked the civil rights movement. That's what we let historians get away with.

I said to her, "Tell me. You tell me what happened."

And when she did, she caught me by surprise. She sounded almost like she was in a trance: "I just couldn't get Emmett Till off my mind," she said.

Rosa was born in 1913 in Tuskegee, Alabama. Her daddy was one angry man because he wanted to be a Garveyite. Garveyites were those black folks who followed Marcus Garvey, a Jamaican-born black nationalist who advocated Pan-Africanism and the economic and political empowerment of blacks. But Marcus Garvey didn't accept light-skinned Negroes, and Rosa's dad was one. So, instead, he had to make do with sitting on his porch with his double-barrel shotgun daring white folks to mess with him.

At the time of the bus incident, Rosa was a secretary for the Montgomery chapter of the NAACP. White folks like to say she was just some tired housewife who didn't want to stand up on the bus that day, but she was no less an activist than Martin Luther King Jr.

In Montgomery, Alabama, where it happened, Negroes had to sit at the back of the bus, behind the white folks. But here's one thing I *didn't* know: they had to get *on* the bus at the front door, pay the fare, and then get *off* and walk to the *back* door. (When black folks got on at the back, they might find white boys in the back flirting with the black sisters, and most of those women would be flirting back, smiling and saying, "Aw, come on, Ed. You don't mean it." But not Rosa Parks—she didn't play that mess. When white boys tried flirting with her, she'd say, "Don't you *ever* say that to me again, you son of a bitch, you.") Also, if you were black and you were sitting in the last row of seats reserved for white folks, and a white person wanted to sit down in that row, in your seat, then the *three other blacks in the same row* had to get up, too. It wasn't just one seat involved. That was segregation for you.

Anyway, a couple of times when Rosa got off the bus to walk to the back door after paying her fare up front, the driver drove off and left her—one driver in particular. When she was describing that famous day to me, Rosa said, "Had I known that was him"— meaning the driver who had given her trouble before—"I wouldn't have got on that bus." But that's the universe at work.

So, there's Rosa sitting in the first row of the colored section when a white guy gets on and there are no free seats in the white section. Later, this man would say, "We were getting off in a couple of stops." So, he wasn't the one trying to make Rosa Parks give up her seat. He figured it wasn't worth the trouble. But the bus driver, the same one Rosa wanted to avoid, went back there and called her a nigger bitch and told her to get up.

But Rosa wasn't having it. She wasn't just tired, she was *mad as hell* because she was thinking about Emmett Till.

The Montgomery Bus Boycott

Today, you've got cops killing black folks. Over nothing. Just because they're black. Eric Garner, Michael Brown, Tamir Rice, Sandra Bland—too many to name. Our black children, our black husbands, every now and then a black woman. And some black activists are trying to do something, but a lot of black people don't care because they're scared. There's a way to fight back, though, if we would just organize—and think about one word: *retail*.

One-third of all retail sales happen between Thanksgiving and Christmas. In other words, in one month, businesses make a third of all the money they make all year. Now, unless your daddy's a businessman, you probably didn't know that. But now you know. So, if we all said, "Because of these black men being killed, we're calling for a boycott from Thanksgiving through Christmas," if we did that, we would be heard. We've taken this kind of action in the past.

What am I talking about? Down south in the 1950s. The bus boycotts. It started in Montgomery, Alabama, in 1955. Everybody knows Rosa Parks refused to give up her seat on the bus in Montgomery, and that that sparked the bus boycotts. But what some people forget is this: the reason the boycotts worked was because the buses were a *business*, and when they couldn't get black folks' money, they were brought to their knees. We black folks got sick of paying our money for the privilege of being abused by all-white drivers and being told where we could and couldn't sit. Martin Luther King Jr. organized the boycott hoping that 60 percent of black people would participate. Instead, 90 to 100 percent of us did, because we'd had enough. Black folks got together and said, *No more.* And it worked. The bus company gave in to our demands. Then the boycott spread to other cities.

That's what we need to do today. The Montgomery Bus Boycott went on for 381 days, over a year—but I'm only talking about boycotting businesses for one month. We've got to decide what we *want.* Do we want to protect our sons and daughters and husbands and wives and mothers, or do we want to spend money we don't even *have* on stupid toys and then tell our kids they came from a white man named Santa Claus? Do we want our kids to grow up safe, or do we want to freeze our behinds off waiting for stores to open on Black Friday and then trample one another to death trying to get to a pair of sneakers—in the spirit of Christmas?

We all know it would be easier on us all around to just not shop because we know that we don't have the money. We can say that it's for a good reason—protesting police brutality.

Pullman Porters and
the Montgomery Improvement Association

I want to tell you a story about cooperation. It starts back in the nineteenth century.

George Pullman was one smart white guy. In the mid-1860s, just about the time slavery ended, he designed his own line of railroad sleeping cars. Pullman cars. That's not what proved he was smart—any fool could have come up with that. What made George Pullman smart was that he realized he needed folks to work on those cars, and because he was in business, he didn't want to pay those workers more than he had to. So, now, you're looking to hire porters for the sleeping cars, and you want them cheap, and slavery has just breathed its last sorry-assed breath. So, what do you do? Hire black folks!

Yes, that George Pullman was one smart white dude. Well, anyway, you have to admit his timing was good.

He really was smart, though, for this reason: In the nineteenth century, all rich folks were white, but not all white folks were rich. Matter of fact, a lot of them were struggling to get by, some of them not doing too much better than some black folks. The only way those white folks had servants was in their dreams. George Pullman figured it this way: as long as white folks were sleeping in his cars, he'd give them their dreams. If they took an overnight train trip, they could sleep in a Pullman car and pretend for as long as they were on it that they were Massa himself, with a big old, six-foot-three, pearly-white-teethed grinning Negro waiting on them hand and foot.

Now, this wasn't exactly a bargain for the porters. At least, it wasn't *supposed* to be. But show me a Negro, and I'll show you somebody who knows how to turn a messed-up situation to his advantage. By the time the porters finished paying for their own uniforms and for the polish that went on *white folks' shoes*, they may not have had two dimes to rub together from their salaries. Still, they got paid in something else: information from folks who forgot those six-foot-three-inch, pitch-black, silent, grinning men had ears—and brains. Hell, they forgot they were there at *all*. Those Negroes may as well have been invisible. The white folks got to talking about how the stock market was going to be fixed, and other tidbits about Wall Street, and the porters took that information and what little money they had and they made a killing. That's why so many of the Pullman porters died millionaires and so many of their children finished college. Thurgood Marshall? Dad was a Pullman porter. Meanwhile, if you were a porter, and you recommended your son or nephew, he could be one, too. One leaves, another comes in. It was the closest thing black folks had to an inheritance. And it kept on, into the twentieth century.

Now, watch this here. The porters had a problem, because when they came south, they couldn't stay in hotels, couldn't go to restaurants—good old Jim Crow in action. So, black folks down south would put them up. Meanwhile, after Rosa Parks did what she did, E. D. Nixon and other folks in Montgomery formed the Montgomery Improvement Association to boycott the bus system. When word of the boycott got out, folks from around the world sent money to the association to support it, but white bankers wouldn't open an account for the association to put the money in. Now, you might say, what kind of banker doesn't want money in his bank? That's how much white supremacists hated black folks. So the association gave the money to Pullman porters to deposit in a bank up north! That's how those millions of dollars got into the movement. That's what we can do when we work together.

Cooperation, man.

The Little Rock Nine

Melba Pattillo Beals, Minnijean Brown, Elizabeth Eckford, Ernest Green, Gloria Ray Karlmark, Carlotta Walls LaNier, Thelma Mothershed, Terrence Roberts, Jefferson Thomas—these nine were a lot like Jackie Robinson when he integrated Major League Baseball. Just like Jackie, they were sent into a place where they would be the only black people. Just like Jackie, they were chosen because they were good at what they did. And just like Jackie, they were told they couldn't fight back if anybody gave them trouble. Difference was, Jackie was a grown man when he did what he did, and the nine I've just named were all in their teens in 1957, the year they integrated Little Rock Central High School in Arkansas. They were kids. That was a lot to put on some kids, even if they *were* brave—and they were.

If they were brave, other folks were acting like fools, or worse. In 1954, the U.S. Supreme Court had ruled that segregation in public schools was unconstitutional, but after that, it wasn't like the all-white schools were in a race to see who could integrate first. It took the NAACP to get in people's faces and demand desegregation. That was how the school board in Little Rock came up with its plan to integrate Central High first and then move on to some junior high schools. It chose the nine black students because they had good grades and good attendance records.

The nine showed up at the school on September 4, and all hell broke loose.

The governor of Arkansas was Orval Faubus. Now, you would have thought those nine students were the love children of Godzilla and King Kong the way Faubus reacted to them. He didn't just say he didn't want them in the school—he called out the Arkansas National Guard to make sure they didn't get in. Not that he needed to: the day the nine tried to enter the school, racist whites lined the streets holding signs, yelling all kinds of hateful stuff, and even spitting in those poor kids' faces. Those nine kids weren't monsters, but for that mob, they represented something just as scary: the idea that black kids were just as good as their kids, that blacks were people just like them. A world without somebody to look down on was just too horrible for those white folks to think about.

Well, what happened in Little Rock made news all over the country. Dwight Eisenhower, "Ike," was president at the time, and when the whole nation saw what was going on down there, he was forced to act. He federalized the Arkansas National Guard, meaning that instead of doing what Faubus told them to do, they had to do what *Ike* said. So, now, instead of blocking the students from going into the school, the Guard had to protect them from the angry mob. Then Ike went one better than that and sent in the 101st Airborne Division of the U.S. Army, minus its black soldiers. (Ike must've figured that if the whites in Little Rock saw a bunch of uniformed black folks coming at them, there would be another Civil War.) After twenty days, the nine students were finally able to attend school, but it wasn't as if their problems were over. White students harassed them like it was their job, and most of the time, the National Guard, who had been sent inside the school to protect the nine students, didn't do a thing. At an age when kids should be thinking about who's going to be their prom date and what colleges they might apply to, those nine students had to wake up every morning knowing they had to attend a school full of folks who hated them.

Just like Jackie Robinson, the Little Rock Nine made a sacrifice for others. Those kids served their country as much as any soldier. That's why, in 1999, President Bill Clinton gave each of them the Congressional Gold Medal.

We have fought a great deal for education. I find it astounding that young people randomly drop out of school these days because "The teacher doesn't like me" and other nonsense. Trust me, freedom is found in education.

The contributions made by the Little Rock Nine are also a testament to the effectiveness of the NAACP because they trained those nine. If not for that training, they wouldn't have made it. That's the power and greatness of the NAACP.

Desegregating Lunch Counters

Desegregating lunch counters in 1960—that was done by young people, too. But they weren't from the NAACP, even though the NAACP was putting up the bail when those young people got arrested. No, these were youngsters going in there on their own— college students who had been inspired by Martin Luther King Jr.'s nonviolent protests.

They didn't just decide one day to go into those establishments and sit down. They first had to learn *how to do it*. Activists like James Lawson trained them, teaching them how to sit still at the counters while white folks cussed at them, called them names, or worse—hit them, threw raw eggs at them. Believe me, that stuff is not easy. Our instinct would be to fight, or maybe to run—but to just sit there? That took some serious discipline. Not to mention guts. Those young people knew they could die.

One thing: as an American, you've been taught to fight back. So, how long does it take to train a person so he goes from not taking stuff from anybody to saying, "I gotta take some stuff off white folks, but I'm not gonna hit them back"?

So, when the activists went to the Woolworth lunch counter in Greensboro, North Carolina, and sat there, they knew what to expect. There were four of them at first: Ezell Blair Jr., Franklin McCain, Joseph McNeil, and David Richmond, all students at North Carolina Agricultural and Technical State University. Soon they would be called the Greensboro Four.

The first day, the four of them sat at the counter and asked politely for coffee. The servers said no, and the manager asked them to leave. But the four stayed until the place closed that night.

The next day, they went back, and twenty other black students from different schools joined them. By that time, there were newspaper reporters and a TV camera present. Third day, sixty people. Fourth day, more than three hundred. A few days after that, the lunch counter protest spread to others southern cities, like Richmond, Virginia, and Nashville, Tennessee. Meanwhile, people boycotted other stores in Greensboro with segregated lunch counters, and it cut into the stores' profits so bad that the managers said, "To hell with it"—and desegregated the lunch counters.

The same approach worked when it came to black folks traveling on integrated buses. They'd get on the buses, racist whites would stop the buses, and the Ku Klux Klan would be waiting to whup them—and those brave, disciplined young people just took it. Then, all at once, the stories started hitting the papers, and readers were embarrassed to see people beating on folks who weren't fighting back. That's how people's minds, and the laws, got changed. Through young black people's bravery. And messing with folks' money a bit.

Dorothy Height and the National Council of Negro Women

Dorothy Height was president of the National Council of Negro Women. She was born in Virginia in 1912. When she was young, her family moved to Pennsylvania, and she went to integrated schools. She was so good at speaking that she won a national competition in high school that got her a college scholarship. She was on her way.

Barnard College, in New York City, accepted her and then changed its mind. It took only two black students a year, and apparently, it already had its two. Height didn't let this discourage her, though. She enrolled at New York University and got her bachelor's and master's degrees there.

At twenty-five, she joined the National Council of Negro Women, which was started in 1935 by Mary McLeod Bethune, who figured that there were so many organizations for black women around the country that they needed to talk to one another a little bit. That's what the council was for. Bethune was the first woman to run it, and then she handed it off to Dorothy Ferebee; next after that was Vivian Carter Mason. And then, in 1957, just when things were heating up good with the civil rights movement and all the folks opposed to it, Dorothy Height took over the organization. She couldn't have picked a tougher or more exciting time to do it.

When we black folks started demanding our rights in the South, things turned violent—black and white folks got beaten, arrested, killed. Height took a peaceful approach to the whole thing. She arranged for what she called "Wednesdays in Mississippi." Groups of women of different races went around together in the summer of 1964 to try to improve how blacks and whites related to one another and to help with voter registration.

Now, if it wasn't bad enough that she had to watch black people get mistreated, she also had *her own people* mistreating *her*. Even though she was in charge of a major civil rights organization, and even though she helped organize the 1963 March on Washington, black men didn't ask her to speak at it. She was standing right there, near Martin Luther King Jr. when he was giving his "I Have a Dream" speech, and she didn't get to say a word.

One civil rights leader, James Farmer, even admitted it. He later called Height one of the "Big Six" in the civil rights movement (along with King, Farmer, John Lewis, Roy Wilkins, and Whitney Young), but said she didn't get credit because she was a woman. (Sure enough, a lot of people put A. Philip Randolph in the Big Six instead of Height.) And don't think she wasn't aware of it herself. She said the men in the group "were happy to include women in the human family, but there was no question as to who headed the household."

Whatever list she was or wasn't on, Height made herself and her organization heard. She advised President Dwight Eisenhower to integrate schools and leaned on President Lyndon Johnson to place black women in positions in government.

Height was president of the National Council of Negro Women for forty years. Another U.S. president, Bill Clinton, gave her the Presidential Medal of Freedom in 1994, and in 2004 she was awarded the Congressional Gold Medal. She died in 2010—at ninety-eight years old. When he gave her eulogy, President Obama called her the "godmother of civil rights."

In addition to Dorothy Height, there so many other black women who risked their lives, fighting on the front lines, who did not receive their rightful credit. Thank you, thank you, thank you to all of our unsung Sheroes.

Selma

The march in Selma, Alabama, in 1965, was about a civil rights worker named Jimmie Lee Jackson. This church deacon, twenty-six years old, went to vote, and they wouldn't let him. It was about Jimmie Lee . . . and being a turtle. Let me explain.

Remember one thing: 66 million years ago, that big horrible thing, the asteroid bigger than mountains, killed the dinosaurs. That's the information they feed to you, your children, and your grandchildren. What they don't tell you is when the dinosaur was here, so was the turtle, and so was the butterfly. That was 66 million years ago, and the *turtle* and the *butterfly* are still here! Gorgeous, pretty, not evil or mean or horrible. The turtle just makes his way along, real slow. And that's how we won the civil rights movement—we took on the mightiest nation in the history of the planet with no guns, and we did it by becoming turtles: hard on the outside, soft on the inside, and willing to stick our necks out. We need to recognize that as strength.

In February 1965, Jimmie Lee Jackson was part of a march in Marion, Alabama. The marchers were protesting the arrest of another worker, James Orange. Jackson was the leader of the protest. He was a deacon in the church, and fiercely committed to ushering in change. Now, this was a peaceful protest, but the Alabama State Troopers didn't care about "peaceful"; all they heard was "protest," and they thought it was time to bust heads. And worse: the night of the protest, they turned off all the streetlights in the town, and when it was good and dark, the troopers went at those folks with clubs, but not just clubs. The protestors took off running.

As the police were attacking everyone, a number of the demonstrators ran into a convenience store. The police followed, and continued to beat people inside the store. One of those people was Jimmie Lee's grandfather. Jimmie Lee's mother attempted to come to the aid of her father, and the police began to beat her too. When Jimmie Lee tried to protect his mother, the police shot him five times, and instead of taking him to the hospital, they took him to the jail. Eventually he was finally taken to the hospital, where five days later he died from his wounds.

After his funeral, local leaders marched over the Edmond Pettis bridge, to protest the killing of Jimmie Lee. However, they were met with even greater violence from the police. After news of this attack went around the world, both local and national leaders came together to organize a huge voting rights march from Selma to Montgomery.

That's what the march in Selma was about. Wasn't about voting rights. It was about Jimmie Lee Jackson. And when that march happened, that's when all hell broke loose. You go by Jimmie Lee Jackson's grave back then, and they're sitting there with rifles, shooting the tombstone.

FOR THOSE WHO HAVEN'T BEEN TO JAIL BUT KIND OF WONDER in the back of their minds what it was like in the civil rights days, well, let me explain it to you. First day you get arrested, the food is horrible. Second day, it's miserable. The third day, it doesn't taste too bad. The fourth day, you're asking for the recipe.

By the time I got down south to protest, blood was running in the streets.

I left the hotel one night to get a case of whiskey, because I drank with this one state trooper every night. This trooper was a brother—married to a black woman, lived in a black neighborhood, his children went to black schools—but the white folks thought he was white!

So, he came to see me with this look on his face. I said, "What's happening, man? Where's the whiskey?"

He said, "I was at this meeting, man, and tomorrow they've got three hundred white folks who came in from all over the South—they're gonna kill all of y'all. And our job is to rope off the press so they can't get across the street. I'm just thankful I know you, man, so you can tell the folks."

I guess he thought if I told the marchers about the danger, we'd all stay home. I said, "I'm not gonna tell them nothing. I *came* here to die. I don't *want* to die, I *came* here to die. So tomorrow we die."

The next day we were there, and the trooper who had warned me—and who was on duty now and passing for white—looked at me with tears in his eyes, shaking his head, and whispered, "You didn't *tell* them!"

We were there, old black folks, young black folks, singing, "Glory, glory hallelujah . . . My eyes have *seen* the glory." We were marching. Then, at a certain point, we got to one corner and, just like my trooper friend had told me, the troopers had roped off the press. Then, I looked in another direction and saw a whole lot of angry white folks waiting on us. I thought about my wife and my children. But this was war.

I saw that the white mob had pickaxes, rifles, clubs. I thought, "I sure don't want to die. If I'd known this was going to happen, I'd have got me a little *pussy* before I left home!" Then the marchers saw all the armed white folks, but we kept singing and we kept praying. Most of us didn't know what was fixing to happen.

Then, all of a sudden, I saw those white folks *shaking*. They were *scared*. A look had come over their faces. It was like I had died and gone to another planet. I looked at them, and they dropped their pickaxes. They had this horrible look on their faces, and two years later I figured out what it was: We marchers were out there, unafraid, willing to die but not to kill, and, well, those folks saw the spirit of God in us.

We kept marching, and we kept marching.

Shirley Chisholm Runs for President

Here's a lesson on how people's minds get messed up.

Shirley Chisholm, the first black congresswoman in America, was born in 1924 in Brooklyn, New York. Family didn't have much money. From the ages three to ten, Shirley lived on her grandmother's farm in Barbados, in the Caribbean. Barbados is more than 90 percent black. Think about that: for seven years when she was a small child, which is when your mind and your ideas about the world are forming, she wasn't around anybody but black folks. She didn't see black folks being told they were inferior to white folks or acting like they were. There were almost no white folks around for them to feel inferior *to*. She got to see black folks in charge. Black people in the Caribbean felt differently about themselves. Not like here, where we grow up being told in a hundred different ways that we're no good, and we believe it, and we don't even *know* we believe it.

In her book *Unbought and Unbossed*, Shirley Chisholm writes that Barbados is "a rocky place, not lush like Jamaica or Trinidad." Folks there weren't sitting around sipping piña coladas. They were *serious*. They may have been mostly farmers, but when they went to school, they *learned*. And the ones who came to the United States came with a purpose. Chisholm writes in her book that they all wanted "the same two things: a brownstone house and a college education for their children." And most of them *got* it.

Chisholm certainly got a college education, and then some—studied at Brooklyn College and then got a master's degree at Columbia University. Studied elementary education, and won prizes for debating. She was so good at debating, in fact, that folks told her she should go into politics. Next thing you know, she was in the New York State Assembly, and after that, the U.S. Congress starting in 1968. When she got there, they tried to put her on the agriculture committee. They must have thought the people she represented rode tractors instead of the subway. But Shirley wasn't having it. She told them just what they could do with their agriculture committee—and that's how she got on the education and labor committees, working on stuff people *cared* about.

After that, she ran for president. In fact, she became the first woman Democrat and the first black woman from a major party to do it. Weren't too many folks thinking about a black president in 1972, but as Shirley said, "*Somebody* had to do it first." (See? That's the kind of thinking you can do when you don't feel you're inferior to other folks.) And Shirley didn't just run: in the New Jersey primary, she came out ahead of a white dude named Terry Sanford, who had been governor of North Carolina.

Now, all this tells you what she *did*, but it doesn't tell you who she *was*.

Now, look at this: That same year, 1972, George Wallace ran for president. I'll say this one thing for Wallace: he was honest. He didn't like black folks, and he *told* people he didn't like black folks. When he was the governor of Alabama, his unofficial motto was "Segregation now, segregation tomorrow, segregation forever," and he meant what he said—which was why he went to the University of Alabama in person in 1963 to block black students from getting in there. You hear me? He didn't send in the police. He went there him*self*.

Then, on May 15, 1972, Wallace got shot. He was paralyzed for the rest of his life. While he was in the hospital, you know who went to visit him? Shirley Chisholm. Black people gave her ninety-nine kinds of grief for doing that, but she believed it was the right thing to do. Even Wallace was moved.

He asked her, "What are your people going to say?"

She told him, "I know what they're going to say. But I wouldn't want what happened to you to happen to anyone."

Wallace never did stop crying over that. He was humbled by the African American values Shirley Chisholm was showing: integrity, compassion, kindness.

Jesse Jackson Runs for President

Jessie Jackson probably has one of the most brilliant minds on the planet. A lot of people didn't know his genius till he ran for president, in 1984 and 1988. He surprised a lot of folks then. They didn't think he had a chance, because he was what the media called a "fringe" candidate—not only was he black, but he had never held elected office. But the establishment started paying attention when a whole lot of people voted for him.

Jackson was born in 1941 in South Carolina. His mama wasn't but sixteen years old, and she wasn't married to Jesse's daddy, who was thirty-three (and married to somebody else). Jesse's mother later married another man, and Jesse took his stepfather's last name, Jackson. Even after that, though, Jesse got teased by the other kids because his parents weren't married. The pain of that must have stayed with him. He lived under segregation, too, riding in the back of the bus and all the rest of it. He did all right as a young man, though: got good grades in school and earned letters in football, baseball, and basketball. Went to college, at the University of Illinois and then North Carolina Agricultural and Technical State University. Then he went to the Chicago Theological Seminary and almost got a master's degree, but he got so caught up in the civil rights movement that he left school. He was with Martin Luther King Jr. and James Bevel on the march from Selma to Montgomery.

In 1965 Jackson went to work for the Southern Christian Leadership Conference, the SCLC, and King and Bevel put him in charge of the SCLC's Operation Breadbasket, which was all about getting jobs for black folks. That's where Jesse's brilliance started to come out. In the same way that King had used boycotts, to make it so black folks wouldn't have to ride at the back of the bus anymore, Jackson applied the idea to jobs, organizing boycotts of white-owned businesses to pressure them into hiring more black folks. The plan worked.

After King got killed, Ralph Abernathy took over the SCLC, and he and Jackson clashed like two cymbals. When Abernathy tried to take Operation Breadbasket away from him, Jesse and his whole staff left the SCLC and formed another organization, Operation PUSH—the "PUSH" stood for "People United to Save Humanity," which Jesse later changed to "People United to Serve Humanity."

Jesse would lead rallies, standing there before big crowds of black folks and filling them with pride. He'd raise his fist and shout in that passionate southern voice, "I Am Somebody!" and people would raise their fists and shout it right back at him. Whole stadiums full of people repeating after Jesse, "I am somebody! I may be poor, but I am somebody! I may be on welfare, but I am somebody! I may be unskilled, but I am somebody! I am black! Beautiful! Proud! I must be respected!" I've heard it said that when Jesse was saying, "I am somebody," he was saying it partly to himself—thinking about when he was teased as a boy because his parents weren't married.

Later, Jesse started making a move toward politics. In 1984, he ran for president himself. He stepped down as head of Operation PUSH and formed the Rainbow Coalition. Jesse's whole thing was that oppressed groups—blacks, poor whites, Hispanics, women— needed one another.

Now, here was Jesse, a black man who had never been elected to anything, running for president of the United States! Of course, they didn't take him seriously as a candidate—that is, until he finished up ahead of every officeholding Democrat except Sen. Gary Hart and former vice president Walter Mondale. Mondale ended up losing big to President Reagan that fall. Maybe Jesse hadn't held office before, but the things he was saying meant something to people.

Despite the loss, in 1988 he was back, this time with more money and better organization. Still, he got knocked out by Michael Dukakis (who got his butt kicked in November by George W. Bush's daddy, George H. W. Bush).

By the time he spoke at the 1988 Democratic National Convention, Jesse's candidacy was over—but he gave one hell of a speech. He told the crowd:

> America is not a blanket woven from one thread, one color, one cloth. When I was a child growing up in Greenville, South Carolina, and grandmamma could not afford a blanket, she didn't complain and we did not freeze. Instead she took pieces of old cloth—patches, wool, silk, gabardine, crockersack—only patches, barely good enough to wipe off your shoes with. But they didn't stay that way very

long. With sturdy hands and a strong cord, she sewed them together into a quilt, a thing of beauty and power and culture. Now, Democrats, we must build such a quilt.

Farmers, you seek fair prices and you are right—but you cannot stand alone. Your patch is not big enough.

Workers, you fight for fair wages, you are right—but your patch labor is not big enough.

Women, you seek comparable worth and pay equity, you are right—but your patch is not big enough.

Women, mothers, who seek Head Start, and day care and prenatal care on the front side of life, relevant jail care and welfare on the back side of life, you are right—but your patch is not big enough.

Students, you seek scholarships, you are right—but your patch is not big enough.

Blacks and Hispanics, when we fight for civil rights, we are right—but our patch is not big enough.

Gays and lesbians, when you fight against discrimination and a cure for AIDS, you are right—but your patch is not big enough.

Conservatives and progressives, when you fight for what you believe, right wing, left wing, hawk, dove, you are right from your point of view, but your point of view is not enough.

But don't despair. Be as wise as my grandmamma. Pull the patches and the pieces together, bound by a common thread. When we form a great quilt of unity and common ground, we'll have the power to bring about health care and housing and jobs and education and hope to our nation.

We, the people, can win.

The Million Man March

Here's how I knew the Million Man March was going to be a success: Before it was held, I was coming off a thirty-day fast in Los Angeles. I don't know what got into me. I walked up this hill to go to the store to get me some bottled water, and I was so weak from the fast that that walk up the hill was kicking my behind. Then a guy from across the street called out, "Dick Gregory!" He got off a ladder and ran over to me. I told him, "Help me with this water." He said, "I got my ticket to go to the Million Man March."

This was *four months before the march.* That's when I knew how big it was going to be.

The march took place on October 16, 1995. The idea for it had come from Louis Farrakhan, the head of the Nation of Islam, but he worked with a number of groups to make it happen. The thinking behind it was that black men would come together from all over as a show of unity, to commit to doing better as men and husbands and fathers, to demonstrate to the nation that the people thought of as criminals could gather in an orderly and peaceful way, and to draw attention to the problems facing the black community. With unemployment, mass incarceration, and the Reagan administration's cuts to any kind of program aimed at helping folks in poor communities, things were getting to a crisis stage for black people.

Farrakhan was a lot of things before he was the organizer of the Million Man March. He was born Louis Eugene Walcott in 1933 in the Bronx. At eighteen, he went south to attend a teachers' college, but he loved music so much he tried his hand at that instead—he could sing and play the violin like nobody's business. Sang calypso. They used to call him the Charmer. Later, in the 1950s, he got into activism, and in Chicago he joined the Nation of Islam. Just like Malcolm X had given up his original surname, "Little," Farrakhan became "Louis X" for a while; after all, "Walcott" was a slave master's name. Then Elijah Muhammad, head of the Nation of Islam, gave him the last name "Farrakhan."

Farrakhan worked with Malcolm X in Harlem, and then took over Temple No. 7 after Malcolm's break with the Nation. He had a lot of Malcolm's charisma. After Elijah Muhammad died, Farrakhan thought he was going to take over the Nation, but Elijah's son Wallace became the new head. Wallace broke away from black nationalism and was all about traditional Islam instead. At that point, Farrakhan broke off and started *another* Nation of Islam, more like the one Elijah had overseen.

A lot of famous people spoke at the Million Man March— Jesse Jackson, Maya Angelou, Martin Luther King III, Benjamin Chavis, Rosa Parks, and Farrakhan—but the vast majority of the people there were just ordinary folks coming together. Farrakhan called it a "Day of Atonement," because as much as we were telling others that things had to improve, we were also telling *ourselves* that *we* had to improve.

And calling it the Million Man March? That shows you the kind of thinking we need. Farrakhan and the rest didn't wait for the media to say that there were a million people there that day. They *made* it a million! I met with Farrakhan and sat with him a while. I said to him, "Did you trademark the name 'Million Man March'? Because if you didn't, the Ku Klux Klan can trademark it now, and you can't use it."

I took my three sons to the march with me. We got up at four o'clock in the morning to go. Ninety percent of the people who came didn't have hotel rooms, because the hotels were full. You had brothers flying in from everywhere, man—some came from Europe, with their own planes. *One point nine million people* were there. What I wanted my sons to see, as we walked through the crowd, was that you couldn't smell any marijuana, you didn't see cocaine on anybody's nose, and you didn't smell alcohol. That's how much respect everybody had for the occasion, and they didn't need to take drugs or drink alcohol to feel good that day.

Only two arrests were made the whole day. A white boy called in a bomb threat from Fourteenth and U Streets, and they kept him on the line long enough to trace and arrest him. The other arrest was of a Chinese or Middle Eastern selling hot dogs without a permit. Nothing else. That was it. A beautiful, glorious gathering.

I would put just one march ahead of that, and that was King's March on Washington in 1963, although he had just 250,000 people. Still, that 1963 march was the first time in the history of the planet that all black folks were invited to come to this major city. Not just the rich. Not just the famous. Not just the educated. King said, "All of y'all come." That was something else, man. Blacks folks were so used to being ignored that at first we didn't understand it. "You mean, come to the nation's capital? I'm invited?" They came in their Sunday shoes, bunions and all, and you felt the joy! Joy. And that dirty dog President Kennedy had seven divisions of troops surrounding the march, because they thought there was going to be violence. Why? Because white folks knew that if somebody had been doing them like they'd been doing black folks, well, they'd have burned the city down. But no, man, nothing like that happened. What a glorious day.

The Million Man March, well, that changed brothers' lives. After it, a lot of them joined churches, mosques, the NAACP, and other groups to try to improve our communities. The National Association of Black Social Workers received thousands of applications from people wanting to adopt black children. We proved we could come together.

The Black Lives Matter Movement and Michael Brown

Black Lives Matter. Almost as soon as the phrase was invented, some small-minded people came out and said, "All lives matter." Hmm. How come nobody used "All lives matter" until after *we* had used "Black lives matter"?

You have to look at when the brother Michael Brown was killed in Ferguson in 2014 by the white cop Darren Wilson. I went there afterward. It happened twenty miles from where I was born. I was outraged when I got there and heard the whole story. Here was a man lying bleeding on the ground for four and a half hours, and in all that time, you didn't see an ambulance. You didn't see a car from the coroner's office. But you'd best believe the cops were there, though. You think we don't see through that?

We marched twenty-four hours a day there in Ferguson, around the clock, in protest. Not the same people—different people came, including children. There was never any violence— well, not until after eight o'clock on the night they announced that the grand jury was not going to indict Darren Wilson. I ask you: why'd they wait until after it got dark to read the grand jury's verdict? I'll tell you why. Because they knew that nighttime is when violence can occur.

I was there when that grand jury finding came down. I saw the reaction. I told Marty King, "Get outta here, man. Something's not right about this. Get out."

We black folks can't see through this kind of behavior by white folks, but we'll say to one another, "Oh, we shouldn't use the word *nigger*. We have to use *n-word*." Why did the word *nigger* get changed to *the n-word*? And why were we stupid enough to go along with it? The word got changed because of the O. J. Simpson trial. There are millions of people who believe that O. J. Simpson killed his wife and Ron Goldman. And they believe Detective Mark Fuhrman's racist statements, and his use of the word *nigger* are why O.J. went free. Then some white person decided it was time to get rid of that word, and we black folks are stupid enough to go along with it. Saying "n-word" is an insult to me. Suppose, one day, men feel bad because of the way we have raped women, and those of us who *didn't* rape them feel bad because we sat by and didn't say anything, and so we decide to change *rape* to *the R-word*. That's an insult.

Dorian Johnson was Michael Brown's best friend and had been present at his shooting. Johnson said that Brown's hands were up when Darren Wilson shot him. Saying that is not a federal crime, so why are people saying the FBI put him under witness protection? Because he was testifying to the grand jury. Turns out he lied. Here's a man who was lying about Michael Brown's "hands up" stance, and on the night the grand jury decision came down, *his* friend DeAndre Joshua was murdered. He was shot and his body burned up in a car. That was *Johnson's friend*. But more important than that, Joshua was killed two blocks from where the prosecutor read the announcement about the grand jury decision. And nobody talks about it. That's what this is about. So, when you stop and look at what they do and how they do it, then you've got to say, *Hey, something's not right*.

Now, let's look at the prosecuting attorney, Robert McCulloch. If you're a white prosecuting attorney anywhere in America, and you're elected by a county that's predominantly white, and you have to send your children to school with their children, and you have a mortgage to pay and all kinds of other responsibilities—are you really going to try very hard to win an indictment for a white cop when you've got to go to those same folks to get reelected? What kind of fool would you have to be to do that? And we're surprised when McCulloch prosecutes a grand jury case that doesn't lead to Darren Wilson's indictment? Are we fools, too?

Obama

First, when it comes to President Barack Obama, I have to apologize to white folks. I mean it. Up until Obama became president, I really believed that all white folks thought all black folks looked alike. But after Obama got in office, I didn't have a single white person run up to me and say, "'Scuse me, Mr. President."

I really want to believe Obama's smart, but to let somebody put you in charge of a raggedy old, broke-down, evil, hateful, ungodly, unspiritual system of government like the one in this country, you've got to be a fool. I mean, please. After Obama was elected, he called me and asked, "What must I do?" I said, "Ask for a recount."

But here is how Obama changed things around the world:

If you've been following the G8 and G20 meetings all over the world for the last twenty years, you've seen that white children have shown up outside those meetings, and whoever was the U.S. president at the time, they'd hang and burn him in effigy. But in London, when Obama was flown in, they didn't hang him in effigy, because they were sensitive enough to know how many black Americans had been lynched throughout history. Now, how is it that foreigners are sensitive to something that whites at home don't appear to be?

Here at home, the white supremacy and double standards haven't gone anywhere. We've got one set of rules for black folks and another set for white folks and another set for women. You could see it even before Obama got elected, when he was running for president. Remember when he was campaigning and it came out that his pastor, Jeremiah Wright, had made some controversial comments? They asked Obama, "Well, how come you didn't leave the church?" Now, Obama's kind and nice, and he responded in a kind and nice way, but if they had asked *me* that, I'd have said, "Well, I didn't see any Catholic priests and nuns leave the Church when the priests got caught abusing those little boys. So, why have I got to be different?" Even Hillary Clinton asked why Obama hadn't left Jeremiah Wright's church. I got on the radio and said, "Miss Hillary, whatever Reverend Wright got caught doing, he wasn't breaking a law, but what your husband got caught doing, lying to a grand jury and obstruction of justice, *that* was a violation of the law, and he insulted and shamed you and your daughter around the world, but *you didn't leave him.*" So, the rules change depending on who you are. Even Obama couldn't change that.

One thing he did change, though—and it'll stay changed, even with Trump in the White House, even with the way folks disrespected Obama, even with the way they want to undo his legacy, Obamacare, and all the rest. Before Obama, whatever white folks didn't have, at least they could take comfort in not being black. To them, a black person was nothing. Before Obama, if I had waved a magic wand that made all white folks dirt poor with no education, unable to read or write, living hand to mouth off the land, those dirt-poor white folks could at least say, "Well, at least I ain't no nigger." Now that a "nigger" has been president, it doesn't help them to say that anymore.

Barack Obama's Presidency

Here's one of the things that is important about Barack Obama's presidency. If you were a black child and were eight years old at the end of it, that means that from the time you were born until 2016, all you ever knew was that a man who looked like you had the most powerful job in the history of the planet. Then Obama leaves office, and a white person becomes president. So, you could say, "Mama, I didn't know a white person could be a president of the United States."

3

The More Things Change, the More They Stay the Same

To tell the truth, that's how a lot of race progress has been made in America. The country gets shamed into doing things it doesn't want to do.

S ome folks say that history works in cycles. Things change all the time, but decades later you can look back to a certain point, and what you're looking at feels the same as what you're going through. In this chapter I give one example of that, involving George Wallace and Donald Trump.

Now, there's no denying that black folks have made a lot of progress in America over the centuries. (Of course, some people will point to that progress and say, "Look, it's better than it *was*," and the unspoken message there is, *Stop your complaining*. Brother Malcolm X had a good response to that: "You don't stick a knife into a man's back nine inches, pull it out six inches, and call it progress.") But it does seem that for every advance black people make, something comes along to make us wonder if we're really going anywhere at all. And that can make you feel discouraged. Sometimes it seems we have to fight not to go forward but just to hold on to what we have. And you know something? That's exactly right. But if we keep fighting, maybe—just maybe—we can take care of that extra three inches, and then see about treating the wound.

Plessy v. Ferguson

People are strange, and racists have got to be the strangest ones of all. You never saw a group of people say one thing and do another so much in your life. Sometimes racists don't seem so much evil as just plain crazy. Sometimes.

Take segregation. Since the first black folks came to America, we've been every shade, from the blackest black to almost pure white. You want me to tell you why? Here's one reason: slave owners couldn't keep their hands off slave women to save their lives. They might not have *said* they were doing it, but the evidence was walking around for everybody to see. Everybody knew what was going on—or should have known. So, when nobody was looking, white folks were all for integration—you couldn't get more integrated than *that*—but when it came to public spaces, they called for separation and segregation like a little baby hollering for his mama.

Here's an example. In 1890, Louisiana passed the Separate Car Act. That meant blacks and whites had to ride in separate cars on railroads. A group of folks in New Orleans, blacks and whites, were against the act. The railroad company was against it, too—not necessarily because it loved black folks, but because it didn't want to spend the money to have extra train cars. So, together they came up with a plan.

Here's something a lot of folks don't understand. Would you have gotten into a boxing ring against Muhammad Ali or Mike Tyson without spending one minute training? Hell no, you wouldn't, not if you wanted to live to see another day. But folks think protestors just wake up one morning and say, "Think I'll go change the world today," and then go out and get themselves thrown in jail. They think Rosa Parks was just too tired to give up her seat, so she said, "Screw it, I'm staying right here. Call Martin Luther King."

No. Protestors *plan* the things they do.

The group in New Orleans, the Citizens' Committee, talked a mixed-race man named Homer Plessey into getting onto a white train car in Louisiana. They even hired a detective to find Plessy on the train and arrest him. Now, the Fourteenth Amendment, which had been passed in 1868, overturning the Dred Scott decision, said that black folks born in the United States were citizens. After Plessy was arrested, the Citizens' Committee, as planned, sued the State of Louisiana, saying that arresting Plessy because of the Separate Car Act was a violation of the Fourteenth Amendment. Never mind that it was the committee that got him arrested in the first place. Slick, right? That's called *planning*. That's the difference between a group of activists and a mob.

It wasn't quite slick enough, though. Two courts in Louisiana ruled against Plessy. Then the Citizens' Committee took the case to the U.S. Supreme Court, which did the same thing. The Supreme Court said that just because blacks and whites had separate facilities, that didn't mean one was better than the other. And that decision made "separate but equal" the law of the land, whether everything was equal or not—which it most definitely was not.

But here's the thing: the kind of planning that went into getting Plessy arrested and bringing a lawsuit is the same kind of planning that went into the civil rights movement in the next century—and this time, it worked better. And almost one hundred years after the Dred Scott decision, "separate but equal" got overturned with the decision in *Brown v. Board of Education of Topeka, Kansas*, in 1954.

What does that tell you? That change is slow, but if you keep fighting, it *does* come.

The Tuskegee Airmen

The Tuskegee Airmen are like storybook heroes. With Hitler on the rise in Germany, the United States started thinking about how it could get ready in case things heated up over in Europe. Late in 1938, President Franklin Roosevelt announced that the government would pay to train pilots near some colleges and universities. That's how the Civilian Pilot Training Program got set up. At first, the military wasn't too excited about it. What good were civilians? Then Germany invaded Poland in 1939, which started World War II, and the military started thinking it might need some help after all. One of the schools where the training was taking place—matter of fact, the main one—was the all-black Tuskegee Institute. Pilots there started training in 1941. In December of that year, the Japanese attacked the U.S. military base at Pearl Harbor, and the United States was in the war for real. Tuskegee trained more than nine hundred pilots, and almost half of them saw combat.

Now, keep in mind, this was the 1940s, and for black folks, it wasn't as simple as just learning to fly and then going over to fight. Jim Crow was an old man by then, but he was still alive and well.

The Tuskegee Airmen were trained by white officers. Those black folks were learning how to fly, but the air force wouldn't give them bombs to practice with, so they took tin cans instead and dropped them by hand. Then they integrated the armed forces during World War II. In the Air Force, though, the black flyers could only be *escort* pilots. They had to guard the guys in the *real* Air Force. Then they noticed that out of all those white dudes who had black pilots guarding them, none of them got shot down.

One of the Tuskegee Airmen, Wendell Pruitt out of St. Louis, helped sink an enemy battleship with nothing but a machine gun fired from an airplane. (Later they messed up and named a big St. Louis housing project after him and William L. Igoe, a congressman. And that place became a bloodbath—it seemed like more people got killed there than in Vietnam. Oh, you'd better be careful what you name things!)

So, now the U.S. Armed Forces and their allies were getting ready for D-day, the invasion of France to free Europe from the Nazis. That was the big thing. So, they go to Gen. Curtis LeMay, the Air Force strategist, and they say, "Say, we've got a problem. There's an Italian castle that we can't get by; they shoot everything down. So, we have to either postpone D-day or find another way in, and there's no other way." LeMay said, "You came to the right man. I've got a group of boys who can drop a bomb through a window." He was talking about the Tuskegee Airmen. If those brothers hadn't blown up that castle, there wouldn't have been a D-day.

Before it was all over, black pilots had flown in nine squadrons in World War II. Benjamin O. Davis, a black man, led the 332nd Fighter Group. They went on 179 bomber escort missions and shot down more than 100 enemy aircraft. They helped beat Hitler, which means they helped save the whole world.

Medgar Evers's Murder

Medgar—there was nobody like him. He was almost in a separate category of human being: so kind, so humble, and so dedicated to the movement and to his people. He was born in 1925 in Mississippi, and wasn't but thirty-seven when he was murdered in 1963, but in his short life, he led the Mississippi NAACP, fought for voting rights and voter registration, and inspired a whole lot of folks. Being with him, I fell in love with the church movement in the South, the voting rights campaign down there, the whole thing.

That movement got so strong. You know that didn't sit right with racists. So, one night when I was down there, I said to Medgar, "Man, I think somethin's going to happen. It doesn't feel right." White folks had strange looks on their faces.

Before something could happen, though, Medgar called me—I was staying at a black minister's house—and said, "Man, you need to call home. Your wife just called."

I said I'd do it later.

He said, "No, it's important, man."

I told him, "I think the white folks are gettin' ready to throw a bomb or something, and I ain't leavin' nowhere."

Medgar knew that my son Richard Jr., two months old, had just died, but he didn't want to tell me. He just wanted me to call home.

He said, "Greg, your son's sick."

I said, "So what."

"Greg, he's dead."

I flew home to Chicago to be with my wife. She was in shock. Eventually I was, too. But soon after, I went back to Mississippi.

Now, here is how the universe works. My plane back to Mississippi got in late, and I had to perform in Chicago later, so I had to leave Medgar's house earlier than planned. Well, Byron De La Beckwith was waiting to kill us at Medgar's house. De La Beckwith was a member of the White Citizens' Council, which had sprung up after the U.S. Supreme Court said in 1954 that school segregation was unconstitutional. The only reason I'm not dead is that my son died and my flight back to Mississippi was delayed.

Before I left Medgar that day, I hugged him and said, "Man, I'm sorry I don't get to die with you. I love you, man."

He knew he was going to be killed. He even knew who was going to do it.

De La Beckwith went free after two trials in 1964 when all-male, all-white juries failed to convict him.

Now, let me fast-forward.

How did De La Beckwith get money? Well, his daddy was a postmaster. Now, President Kennedy, out of all the land to buy for a post office, bought *his* land—for fifty grand. That's how De La Beckwith had the money to pay. Kennedy was one of these low-down dogs whom black folks don't know anything about but like, because they can't spot a racist when he's smiling and putting on a big show of loving black folks. They can't tell the difference between a good white person and a bad one.

Why do I say Kennedy was a low-down dog? When they cut off food stamps in Mississippi, in retaliation for voter registration drives, it had Kennedy's blessing. When that happened, I went back to Mississippi and said, "I'll pick up the tab. I'll send seven tons of food every two weeks. I'll pay for it." And the Kennedy boys—and I didn't know this until Cathy Hughes and TV One did a show called *Unsung*, and I don't know where she got the tapes—you can hear them saying, "We've got to send food stamps again, because that Dick Gregory is getting too much worldwide attention."

But let me fast-forward again. Medgar's widow, Myrlie Evers-Williams, pushed and pushed until she got a new trial for Medgar's murderer. They tried De La Beckwith again in 1994. This time he went to prison, where he died at age eighty in 2001.

A lot of evil went down in Mississippi, but some good happened, too, because of one man: Medgar Evers.

Four Little Girls Killed in the Birmingham Church Bombing of 1963

Carol Denise McNair was eleven years old when she died on September 15, 1963, and Addie Mae Collins, Carole Robertson, and Cynthia Wesley weren't but fourteen. All four of them were murdered, and if their murder wasn't the lowest act ever committed in this country, I don't want to think about what was. Four so-called men from the Ku Klux Klan planted dynamite under the front steps of the 16th Street Baptist Church in Birmingham, Alabama. Blew the girls' bodies apart.

If somebody asks you what "cowardly" means, tell them that story. If the four Klan members had really been men, they would at least have attacked the grown black folks they had problems with. Then again, they've got a problem with *all* black folks, men, women, and children. That's why they're Ku-Kluxers, not men.

The Klan was very strategic; it wasn't just any black church they bombed. Black folks had done a lot of organizing there. James Bevel and the Southern Christian Leadership Conference had put together the Children's Crusade there in May 1963. (That was when more than a thousand students went on a march to challenge the mayor on integration.) Martin Luther King Jr., Ralph Abernathy, and many other civil rights leaders met at the church to plan voter registration drives.

The Klan members probably didn't plan it this way, but what they did helped a lot of people finally see what was happening to black folks, and *that* helped get civil rights law passed—at one hell of a price.

Over time, the bombing demonstrated something else: how much had changed in a few years. Right after the bombing took place, the FBI investigated it, but what's the point of sending one bunch of racists to catch another bunch? The local police in Birmingham had the names of the four from the Klan who they thought had done it, and they gave the names to the FBI. But the FBI director at the time was J. Edgar Hoover, and if black folks ever had a worse enemy than *that* son of a—I take it back. We never did. Hoover blocked the prosecution of the four Klan members and closed the FBI investigation. And that was it.

Or, that *seemed* to be it—until eight years later, when a man named Bill Baxley became attorney general of Alabama. He was just a law student at the time of the bombing, so there wasn't much he could do then, but as attorney general, he reopened the church bombing case and got access to the original FBI files. That's when he found out that the FBI had had evidence it didn't provide to the original prosecutors in Birmingham.

It took six years to convict the first of the accused Klan members, in 1977, and it took until 2000 to nail two more. The fourth one had died already. Two of the others died in prison.

You can do what you want in this life, but the universe *will* get around to you.

Passage of the Civil Rights Act, 1964

Well, the Civil Rights Act of 1964 did one big thing: it put a law between us black folks and racist craziness. For example, if you were running a program that operated on money from the government, and you were even *thinking* about discriminating against black folks, that law said: you don't get federal money if you can't prove you've done this, this, and this. That made a big, big difference. People might say, "I'm opening up my organization to all people out of the graciousness of my heart," and maybe they were, but mainly it was because they wouldn't get federal contracts if they *didn't* do so. The Civil Rights Act made it illegal to discriminate against anybody in public facilities. Made it so blacks and whites didn't have to use separate bathrooms, drink out of separate water fountains. It set up the Equal Employment Opportunity Commission to prevent discrimination in the workplace, and it gave the attorney general the power to protect people from racism in everything from education to voting. So, there's nothing you can compare to the Civil Rights Act. Ninety-nine percent of blacks' current success came from that law.

Except, it didn't happen just like that. And a lot of what made it happen had to do with things going on down South.

Martin Luther King Jr. called Birmingham the most segregated city in America. So, he and others set out to desegregate it. He ran the Southern Christian Leadership Conference, which led the fight to end segregation. The SCLC put together boycotts of businesses that wouldn't hire blacks, and trained high school and college students to sit at segregated lunch counters. Let me tell you, those were some brave young men and women—sitting there calmly while white folks did anything they wanted to them. But what really got folks' attention was the 1963 protest march from the 16th Street Baptist Church to Birmingham City Hall. Well, the head of the Birmingham Police Department, Eugene "Bull" Connor, didn't like that one bit. He had the police use fire hoses and attack dogs on those poor young people, and folks all over the country saw it on television. The world, too.

Now, before that, in 1960, John F. Kennedy had been elected president. He came into office with promises to back civil rights, but he took his time getting around to it. When that mess happened in Birmingham, though, he saw that he had to do something, so he proposed the Civil Rights Act. There were two problems, though. One: it had to get through Congress, and when it comes to being discriminatory, the Congress we have today doesn't have a thing on the one back then. And two: even if Congress passed the legislation, President Kennedy wasn't around to sign it. The same year as the Birmingham protests, Kennedy was assassinated.

That made his vice president, Lyndon Baines Johnson, president of the United States. Now, Johnson was a southerner, but he was a southerner who wanted to do something for black folks. Now the problem was to get the bill past the racist congressmen from the southern states. When they brought the bill to the floor of Congress for debate, the southerners filibustered—getting up and talking trash to run out the clock and kill the bill. But Democratic senator Hubert Humphrey, who was backing the bill, figured out that he had enough votes for Congress to end the filibuster, and that's what they did. And Johnson signed the Civil Rights Act into law on July 2, 1964, with Martin Luther King Jr. standing right behind him.

The Civil Rights Act brought a new day for black folks. But something else happened, too: what they call a white backlash. Some white folks got resentful, and even violent, when the Civil Rights Act started getting enforced. And that backlash had a lot to do with the rise of a segregationist presidential candidate, George Wallace. Decades later, we had eight years of a black president—and some folks resented *that* so much that the next thing we knew . . .

The more things change, the more they stay the same.

Passage of the Voting Rights Act, 1965

The Voting Rights Act—its fifty-year anniversary was celebrated a couple of years ago. That means that if you were thirty years old when it was passed, you're over eighty now. Fifty years of voting for some folks. But voting rights, registering to vote—they don't mean a thing if you don't have voter *education*. Why do you think black folks go in and pull one lever—all for Democrats? Because they think, "That way, I can't make a mistake." Nobody knows how to split a ticket because it's rarely explained. It's like being on an airplane when they give the emergency instructions: I always wonder, with all the time people spend at the airport, why the airlines don't have time to teach us how to use that mask then. The airlines spend two seconds on it when you're sitting on the plane, when they could give you a complete tutorial while you're going through the TSA check. The only time I *see* the mask is when there's an emergency, and I'm supposed to learn it *then*? They just tell us: "Jump in the water. The life preserver's under the seat." It's the same with voter education: the government gives people the right to vote but doesn't show them their *options*.

The Democrats couldn't believe that black folk just came out and voted for them every time. They didn't have to spend any money getting our votes. When the Democrats lost the Senate and the House in 2010, nobody should have been surprised. Why? Because black folks who should have known better didn't have the integrity to pressure Democrats to do anything—to say, "Look. We want two hundred million dollars going to publications on voter education."

Meanwhile, if, fifty years ago, you were age thirty, and you're eighty now, you've got trouble with your bladder, you've got trouble with your memory, yet they don't ask for money for buses with toilets in them to take old folks to where they can vote. Plus, you know how many black folks—and probably white folks, too—die because they forget they've already taken their medication? It's the same thing with voting. Some old folks don't vote because they think they have already.

There should be more voter education, but that doesn't mean the Voting Rights Act isn't important. In some places in the country, mostly the South, it's been the only thing letting some black folks vote at *all*. Congress passed the law, and President Lyndon Johnson signed it on August 6, 1965, but just like any area where black people have made progress, we didn't get it without fighting for it.

A lot of ignorant people look at black folks and say, "Slavery's been over a hundred fifty years. What's the matter with y'all?" What they don't think about is all the obstacles that racists put in place so black folks wouldn't have much more freedom *after* slavery than we had *under* it. The Fifteenth Amendment to the Constitution was supposed to protect our right to vote, but the people who didn't want black folks voting found some ways around that. At first, beginning in the 1860s, right after slavery ended, they used plain old violence to try to keep us away from the polls. Then, in the decades after that, they started to get slick.

It was: "Hey, boy, welcome to the voting booth! Step right up! *Sure*, you can vote! Just a couple of things we've got to get straight first. You own some property, don't you, boy? *No?* Well, then, I'm mighty sorry, but . . ."

Or: "Yeah, gal, come on in! You can vote . . . just as soon as you read this here document with all these fancy words I don't even understand myself and tell me exactly what it all means. Don't make no mistakes, now."

In 1903, in *Giles v. Harris*, the U.S. Supreme Court decided it didn't have the power to force states to register black folks. And that's how things stood for a good long time.

Then came the 1950s and '60s. Along with pushing for everything else, civil rights activists pushed for the federal government to protect black folks' right to vote. In 1965, in Marion, Alabama, activists were having a voting rights march at night, and police came and started busting heads. That night, a young black man, a protestor named Jimmie Lee Jackson, got shot to death. Afterward, Martin Luther King Jr. and James Bevel from the SCLC, and John Lewis and others from the Student Nonviolent Coordinating Committee, or SNCC, organized the marches from Selma to Montgomery. Police on horseback were there to meet them, and maybe if I tell you that that day has been called "Bloody Sunday" ever since you'll have an idea of what happened next. Folks all over the country saw that bloodbath on TV.

Now, with the whole country outraged, black *and* white, the pressure was on President Johnson. He pushed the Voting Rights Act through Congress. And *finally*, black folks had some protections when it came to voting. The Voting Rights Act has different parts. Section 2 makes it so states can't pass any law that results in racial discrimination. Section 5 makes it so nobody can make any changes that affect voting without first going through the U.S. attorney general or the U.S. District Court for the District of Columbia. And Section 4(b) protected black voters against the southern states that were their worst enemies in the 1960s.

Notice for that last one I said "protected," not "protects." That's because the U.S. Supreme Court ruled in 2013, in *Shelby County v. Holder*, that we didn't need Section 4(b) anymore, because "things today aren't like they were in the 1960s." Section 5 is still in place, but Section 5 without Section 4(b) is like a car without wheels. It's still a car, but it can't do the main thing you need it to do.

Whatever is won, we've got to *protect*.

The Assassination of Malcolm X

Malcolm X and Richard Pryor had something in common. They were both so bashful that they'd embarrass you. They'd pull their heads down; couldn't look up at folks. Malcolm X—you would not believe this was the same man who stood before black leaders and spoke truth. Malcolm was always polite, saying "yessir" and "no sir" to everybody—black folks, white folks, and little children.

And I used to believe he was the biggest fool in the world because he'd memorized a dictionary. I'd say, "Why not just carry a dictionary in your hand? Malcolm, touch your hand." I'd say, "Now, if you could open up your head and touch your brain matter, it's soft as cotton. So, if you wouldn't carry a dictionary with this kind of skin you've got on your hand, why would you put it in your damn *head*?"

Malcolm called me the day they killed him. But let me back up. The first time he called me, he said, "Dick Gregory, it's Brother Malcolm." He said, "We'd like to know when can you come down to the mosque." I said, "What time is it now?" Turned out to be 11:00. I said, "Send a car out here. In about a half hour I should be dressed." He said, "Okay."

Then he called back. He said, "Man, I'm sorry. You can't come out here tonight. Ninety-nine percent of your audience is white"— meaning that if my audience knew I was hanging around with him, they wouldn't be my audience anymore. I said, "Malcolm, send a car out here to pick me up, bring me to the mosque, and we'll stand in front of the mosque and take a picture, and I want it on the front page of *Muhammad Speaks*!" And he did it.

Still, I mean, he was just *bashful*.

As I was saying, Malcolm called me the day they killed him, February 21, 1965. He said, "Brother Greg, you comin' by today?" I said, "Malcolm, I love you. I love you so much, I don't even want to take a chance to be there"—because I knew the government was going to kill him. He said, "What do you mean, Brother Greg?" I said, "Well, I close tonight at Basin Street East, but I had my wife book me a flight into Chicago at eight o'clock this morning, and I had them book me into a college about ten miles from the airport, way beneath my salary. And I'm going to go there and speak this afternoon, and I'm going to stay there until they tell me you're dead. Because I'm not going to let this government get two of us for the price of one. And I'm going to call Adam Clayton Powell when I finish talking to you and beg him not to go there. Because today, the United States government is gonna get you."

Then I went to Chicago, and I was there when they came and told me that Malcolm had been killed.

Malcolm was killed because of another brother, Pio Gama Pinto. Pinto was born in Nairobi, Kenya. He's the one who changed Malcolm's views from black nationalism to Pan-Africanism. He's the one who persuaded Malcolm, when he went to Mecca and stayed seven weeks, to meet with all the *real* leaders of Islam. He was also the one who discussed with Malcolm bringing American racism to the steps of the United Nations. And four days after Malcolm was shot dead in New York City, Pinto was gunned down in Nairobi. Four days! So don't tell me that black Muslims killed Malcolm.

Now, let me show you how this white racist system treats black folks. When the black folks the government hired to kill Malcolm got ready to do it, Malcolm was standing on a stage at the Audubon Ballroom in Harlem. They threw a smoke bomb in the back. When the commotion started, and everybody was going this way and that, the brothers ran up with double-barrel shotguns and shot up at him. Under the Freedom of Information Act, we were able to get the autopsy of Malcolm, and all the bullets in Malcolm were going *downward*. That means the government had such a low view of those black folks that they didn't even give them real bullets; they gave them blanks. Malcolm was shot from *above*. Also under the Freedom of Information Act, we found out the CIA had been forced to admit that it had rented the Audubon Ballroom a week before. CIA agents went in and put those guns in there and shot Malcolm from a downward angle. That's what this game is about.

It's all lies. You know the story about when somebody drove a car by and firebombed Malcolm's house? Now, how're you going to throw something that far, from a car, without stopping? And then the BS when you heard them say, "Yeah, we're lookin for a green such-and-such a car, license plate . . ."

The thing that hurt me was that Malcolm started carrying a gun. I said, "Malcolm, you're fixin' to mess up your legacy. You're not gonna win. Ain't nobody gonna give a damn what you say, and it'll be a thousand years before it sinks in." The message has got to go from a mother and father who were scared of you, to some children who won't be scared of you, and then *their* children, and *their* children, and *their* children.

But Malcolm lived a good life. The Spike Lee movie about him, with Denzel Washington, did not portray that. That movie was an insult. Malcolm's wife, Betty, raised her children, and all while earning a master's and a PhD. The movie didn't have room to tell you that, but it had room to show Malcolm snorting cocaine and having sex with a white woman in a car? It also showed Malcolm putting his head in a toilet? Shameful.

If Malcolm went wrong early in his life, he had a lot of help doing it. He was born in Nebraska in 1925, and when he was just six years old, his father was run over by a streetcar—most likely he was thrown under it by white men. That tore up Malcolm's mother so bad that she ended up in a mental hospital. Malcolm didn't really have a home after that, and he bounced among foster families until he moved to Boston to live with his sister.

And yeah, Malcolm turned to crime after that. At first, he had done well in school, but then a white teacher told him he couldn't

grow up to be a lawyer because he was black. Malcolm lost interest
in school after that. Who wouldn't have? So, in Boston, he started
doing a little bit of everything: pimping, selling dope, breaking into
people's houses. That's what landed him in prison, and prison is
where he learned about the Nation of Islam. By the time he left
prison, in 1952, he had become a follower of Elijah Muhammad.
A couple of years after that, he became the minister of Harlem
Temple No. 7.

Around the time Malcolm started rising in the Nation of Islam, the civil rights movement was getting off the ground. But
Malcolm didn't want anything to do with it because, to him,
the movement was trying to integrate blacks into a corrupt racist society, and he thought black folks would do better on our
own because our traditional values would have enabled us to
thrive—importance of community, love of family, and the like.
He wanted black people to believe in ourselves and be proud of
ourselves, the way he was proud of us. For black people who had
heard all their lives that they weren't anything, Malcolm's words
were like food for the soul. He knew we needed it, just like he
had needed it. What he communicated to black people was: it's
not *right* that you've got to suffer like this. Malcolm was saying
to us: Love yourself! Stand up for yourself! That's why he moved
people so. And as bashful as Malcolm was one on one, you put
him in front of a mic, and that was one charismatic brother. He
could talk. He could *preach*!

Then he began to separate himself from the Nation of Islam,
partly because he was disillusioned by Elijah Muhammad and
partly because he wanted to be more of an activist than he could be
with the Nation. After he visited Mecca in 1964, and met Pinto,
he changed his mind about a lot of things. He no longer believed
all white people were devils, because in Mecca he saw them pray-

ing next to black people, all of them worshipping God together like brothers. He also realized he needed to band together with black people worldwide as well as in America. That's what Pan-Africanism is. When he came back to America, he formed the Organization of Afro-American Unity. He was getting ready to do some big things.

And *that's* when they killed him.

Here's what they couldn't kill, though: the inspiration that brother gave to black folks. A whole lot of people still read Malcolm's speeches and his *Autobiography*, and both give them hope and direction. When they check out the *Autobiography*, they see somebody who went wrong here and there, like maybe they have themselves, but who turned himself around and learned to value himself, to see his own potential. For folks who hear a hundred different ways every day that they don't matter, that's a powerful message. Malcolm was the messenger black folks needed.

Martin Luther King Jr.'s Assassination

Here's the story they tell you about James Earl Ray, the man they say killed Martin Luther King Jr. They say he escaped from the Missouri State Penitentiary, in Jefferson City. Now, never before James Earl Ray and never since has anybody ever escaped from that place. Not even Houdini could have done it. And James Earl Ray was so dumb that he had never committed a crime and not been caught by the cops thirty minutes after he did it. But for almost fifty years they've been saying that this ignorant white boy escaped from the most secure prison in the country and pulled off one of the crimes of the century? Yeah, tell me another one, man.

Here's how it happened—and here's how dumb James Earl Ray was. He's in Missouri State Penitentiary and another white boy, who was part of the *real* group planning to kill King, walks up to him and says, "Hey, James. How'd you like to escape?"

Ray tells him, "Yeah. When we going?"

"*We're* not going—*you* are," the boy tells him. And Ray went for that crap.

This was 1967, the year before King was killed, and Ray was working in the bakery of the penitentiary. They cooked the bread for the prison and a hundred other places—other prisons, state schools, old folks' homes, places like that. When they were done baking the bread, it went into big metal containers, which the guards then loaded onto a truck. If there was a body inside those containers, those guards wouldn't have known the difference. So, on the day of the escape, James Earl Ray was in one of those containers when the trucked pulled off. After a while it stopped on the road near some weeds, and Ray hopped out. Then, to show you how slick this whole thing was, a car just happened to pass by, and Ray got a ride—from the same network of people who had sprung him from prison, the same ones that killed King and pinned it on Ray. But they wouldn't do that for a while yet.

So, this criminal genius, this man they say was later responsible for one of the most famous killings in U.S. history—what did he do next? Messed up everywhere he went, everything he tried. Went to Mexico to make porn movies. Now, you don't have to be a great director to make porn movies. Don't need Shakespearean actors working for you, either. You aim your camera at folks having sex, or *making* like they're having sex, and presto! It doesn't take talent. For it to go wrong, though, you need a special talent for screwing things up, and that's one talent that boy had spilling out his ears. Later, he applied his unique messing-up abilities to being a bartender and even a dancer in Los Angeles.

Finally, after *somebody else* killed King, James Earl Ray made his messing-up way to Canada and then England, and that's where they nabbed him and pinned King's murder on him. Incompetent as he was, the only way he could have killed King was by trying *not* to do it, but this was the dimwit the government sentenced to ninety-nine years in prison for killing the man it wanted to see dead anyway—the man the government itself had had killed.

Now, check this out:

The Lorraine Motel, where King was killed, was nothing but an old whorehouse. What happened was, when King and his lieutenants went south, they had to stay in white-run hotels because the local people were scared they'd lose their jobs if word got out that King was staying with them in their homes. So, King stayed at the Crown Plaza, the Holiday Inn, places like that.

At this time, J. Edgar Hoover, the head of the FBI, was trying to discredit King and mess with him any other way he could think of. When Hoover saw where King was staying, he got the word out to black folks, acting like he was their friend. (With friends like him, black folks could have had an enemy garage sale.) Hoover said something along the lines of, "To My Decent Friends, the Negro People in Memphis: The lying Reverend Martin Luther King had told you to boycott white businesses and he himself stays at the Crown Plaza, Holiday Inn." That meant that King had to move out of the Crown Plaza and into the Lorraine Motel.

Now, the black woman who operated the switchboard at the motel—they say she died from a heart attack when King got shot. How'd she know King had gotten shot if he was out on the balcony and she was inside operating the switchboard? Here's what happened: they killed her so no calls could get out.

Another woman, in the motel office, said that before King checked in, a man had come and told her King would be there that evening and that he didn't like staying on the first floor. "You put him on second floor," the man said. So, they put King on second floor, where he was going to be shot.

Now they have to set up James Earl Ray. They had brought this dummy to Memphis, where he thought he was going to kill King. The plan was that the real assassin would do it and then kill Ray to make it look like he'd been shot after shooting King. Then they would plant evidence on Ray. But they hadn't taken into account Ray's special messing-up superpowers. He was so powerful that way that he could mess up his own plans and other people's, too. At the crucial moment, that nitwit saw that his tire was leaking and went to a filling station to get it fixed. He was still at the filling station when he saw all the cops running around the neighborhood. He got scared, left, and never went back. Later, he got caught at Heathrow Airport, in London—not for killing King, but for the jailbreak. The best part was, when they caught him, in *June*, he was wearing a *coat*. That's the dude they say pulled off one of the crimes of the century—a man so out to lunch that he didn't even know what time of year it was.

That's why you have to question everything they tell you. Grace Stephens, the snaggle-toothed, couldn't-read, couldn't-write, probably black-hating common-law wife of the motel owner—she got put in an insane asylum for saying that the man she saw running from the motel after the shooting *didn't look like James Earl Ray*. Ask yourself why.

And ask yourself this: ever see the photograph of the people at the Lorraine Motel that day, pointing up after the shot rang out? How'd they know where the shot had come from? Let's say you're in a restaurant and a shot rings out. What do you do? Hit the floor, right? Because you don't know if more shots are coming. But here these men are, pointing up like they know what's going on.

Why?

And while you're thinking about that, think about this: In 1993, a white restaurant owner named Loyd Jowers came forward and admitted that he had paid a man to kill Martin Luther King Jr. His restaurant was across the parking lot from the motel where King was killed. He got the money, $100,000, from a man named Frank Liberto, who was in the Memphis Mafia. The man Jowers paid was a lieutenant with the Memphis Police, Earl Clark. After King was shot, a cab driver named Paul Butler saw Clark running from the scene. Butler's mistake was going to the police and telling them what he had seen, because a few hours later, he was as dead as King. What does that tell you? James Earl Ray didn't have a thing to do with killing King, and the plot was bigger than Jowers, Clark, and Liberto. If not, why was Butler killed? Jowers may have been working on behalf of Liberto, and Liberto was part of the Mafia, but what was the Mafia in it for? Why did the Mafia care if King lived or died? Because the Mafia was working for the people who *did* want King dead. Do I have to tell you who they were? The U.S. government.

Think about what King was doing in 1968, the year he got killed. The things he had helped achieve, like the Civil Rights Act of 1964, the Voting Rights Act of 1965, desegregation of bus lines—it didn't change the fact that a lot of people were still living in poverty. They didn't have the basic thing they needed: a living. So, King had decided to take a new approach. He was organizing the Poor People's Campaign. This wasn't about just civil rights. This had to do with all poor people: black, white, Mexican American, Puerto Rican, Native American. The plan was to set up protest camps on the Mall in DC, where the 1963 March on Washington had taken place. Thousands of people were going to occupy the place until they got satisfaction and made a start on getting economic justice. Now, it was one thing when King was stirring up black folks. But if he started stirring everybody else up, too—well, in the eyes of the FBI and the CIA, *that* was going too far. He had become too dangerous.

King's family brought a lawsuit against Jowers, and the half-black, half-white jury decided in *one hour* that Jowers had been involved in killing King. Maybe you never heard about any of this. Why not? Because *the media doesn't tell you everything you ought to know*, and you can't believe everything they *do* tell you. Okay? If you don't remember anything else from this book, remember that.

The Killing of Black Leaders

I want you to think about something. Malcolm X was killed in 1965. Martin Luther King Jr. was killed in 1968. And Fred Hampton, the leader of the Illinois Black Panthers, twenty-one years old, was shot to death in cold blood by the FBI in 1969. What did the three have in common, besides being black leaders? At the time they were killed, they were all reaching beyond the black American community to make ties with other people. That's what the power structure is afraid of: people banding together. And when the power structure is afraid, people die.

Malcolm used to preach one thing: black people being separate from everybody else, on our own and self-sufficient. Then he went to Mecca, and the experience opened his eyes. He started to see the beauty of making common cause with other people. A man he met, Pio Gama Pinto, born in Kenya, led him to think about Pan-Africanism—black people all over the *globe* working together. Then the two of them were killed, *four days apart.*

Martin Luther King Jr. was organizing the Poor People's Campaign. He said, "I think it is necessary for us to realize that we have moved from the era of civil rights to the era of human rights. . . .

We have moved into an era where we are called upon to raise certain basic questions about the whole society." The whole society. Not just black folks. Next thing you know, he had been shot.

Then there was Fred Hampton of the Black Panthers. The Panthers was started in the 1960s by Huey Newton and Bobby Seale to protect black folks from racist police officers. They used to follow the police around, and when the police stopped some black dudes, the Panthers were there to make sure their rights were protected. The Panthers were some badass brothas, wearing their leather jackets and berets. They were all about protecting black folks. But Fred Hampton was starting to move beyond that. He saw that blacks needed to band together with others, and he was starting to make common cause with poor white folks. Go look it up. There's video footage: white Okie-looking dudes you could picture in Klan hoods and robes, except they're standing next to Fred Hampton, saying they stand with the Black Panthers. Next thing you know, Hampton is dead, too.

See a pattern?

Frank Wills and the Watergate Scandal

Let me tell you how a black man who never finished high school brought down the most powerful person on the planet.

In the fall of 1968, Richard M. Nixon was elected the thirty-seventh president of the United States. How he did it was he spent a lot of time on the campaign trail talking about "law and order." Today that's what they call a "dog whistle." The way a dog can hear a dog whistle but people can't—some folks didn't pay attention when Nixon said "law and order," but other folks heard him real good. And those were the ones Nixon was talking to. They knew what Nixon meant by "law and order": *keep black people in their place.*

(When you hear Donald Trump say "law and order," don't think he means anything different.)

Black folks got their revenge on Nixon, though.

Now, Nixon was a Republican, and in 1968 he beat the Democrat, Hubert Humphrey, in one of the closest elections America had ever had. But four years later, in 1972, it was a different story. Nixon was running for reelection, and the Democrats put up George McGovern as their candidate. Maybe the Democrats *wanted* to lose that year. McGovern stood about as much of a chance against Nixon as a cockroach against an elephant. All Nixon had to do to win was not get run over by a bus. But Nixon was insecure—that was his downfall. And his insecurity spread to the people around him.

Some of those people were on what they called the Committee to Re-elect the President, or CRP. In 1972, one of them, G. Gordon Liddy, came up with a plan to break into the Democratic headquarters to photograph documents and plant bugs. That way they'd know what the Democrats were up to and could stop them from winning the election. The plan was illegal, but if you think that kept Liddy awake at night, think again. He told a couple of people about it. One of them was John Dean, who worked as a lawyer for Nixon. The other one was John Mitchell, who was the U.S. attorney general at the time. The attorney general is the top law enforcement officer in the country. How do you like that?

Mitchell didn't like the plan at first, but when a couple of details got changed, he said, "Go 'head." So, Liddy pulled in a couple of other guys, E. Howard Hunt and James McCord, and they got five other dudes to break into the Democratic headquarters, in the Watergate Hotel, in Washington, DC.

Now, here's where the black folks' revenge comes in.

A black man named Frank Wills was twenty-four years old at

the time. He was born in Georgia, and dropped out of high school in the eleventh grade. He went north and found a few jobs, first in Michigan and then in DC. Never made much money. Just an ordinary fella. But that ordinary fella changed history.

In 1972, Wills was working as a security guard at the Watergate. The hotel had to have security guards, but nobody had ever tried to break in, and the place seemed so safe that the building's security guards didn't carry guns. One day, Wills was making his rounds and he noticed a door with some tape over the bolt, put there so the door would close but not lock. Wills took the tape off and went to finish his rounds. A half hour later, he came back around to the same spot, and there was the tape again! Wills knew something fishy when he saw it, so he called the police. That's how the five dudes got arrested while they were trying to spy on the Democrats. When the FBI took a closer look into things, they found out that the five burglars had been paid by CRP. That made the FBI *real* curious.

Now, here's where Nixon blew it. The Watergate break-in wasn't his idea. All he had to do was say, "I ain't have nothin' to do wit' it" and let the FBI look wherever they wanted. But he was scared of what *else* they might find, so that's when the cover-up started. Nixon told one of his aides, Bob Haldeman, to tell the CIA to block the FBI investigation. How do you like that? Two spy organizations working against each other, but they're both working for the same country! Nixon's little plan didn't work, though, and soon a U.S. Senate committee was on his trail. It found out that Nixon secretly taped conversations in his office, and the Supreme Court ruled that Nixon had to turn over those tapes. It was all over then. On the tapes, Nixon could be heard talking about the cover-up.

He knew he was going to get impeached. To avoid that, he

resigned in 1974. His vice president, Spiro Agnew, had already resigned for other reasons, and the new vice president, Gerald Ford, gave Nixon a pardon. He didn't have to do any jail time.

Just about everybody else involved went to jail, though—forty people either went to prison over that Watergate mess or just missed being sent there. All because of one black man: Frank Wills.

Nixon and his boys may have had the last laugh, though. Nixon got away clean, and John Dean, G. Gordon Liddy, E. Howard Hunt, H. R. Haldeman—every last one of those dirty dogs, plus a couple more I haven't mentioned, made serious money writing books about Watergate. What happened to Frank Wills, the only honest one in the bunch and the only one who tried to do his job right? He was fired from his job and was living nearly destitute for a decade. That's how America really treats a true hero. Eventually, I hired him and paid him $2,500 a week. Later, he tried to get a job at Howard University, in DC, but they told him they were scared they'd lose federal funding if they hired him.

I said to Wills one day, "Now, I want to ask you something. Man, when you woke up that morning, you were about to bring down the most powerful human being in the world. Did you feel anything? I mean, did you look up in the sky and see tens of thousands of horses? Did you hear trumpets blow?" I asked him that because I wanted to know: when you get a call like that, do you know something's about to happen? Or do you not know—which means it could happen to any of us?

Buffalo Soldiers

Now, Bob Marley, the Jamaican reggae artist—he was a brilliant musician and songwriter. Brilliant. The minute he opened his mouth and started singing, you'd know it was him, and people all over the world knew him and loved him. Still do. But let me tell you why I first said no to working with him.

One day, I got a message from Bob Marley's office. They wanted to give me forty thousand dollars to be his opening act at Harvard Yard. I told the guy, "Tell him I don't want to work with him." Now, what happened next was kind of interesting, and it showed me the beauty of Bob Marley's humanity. He got on a plane and flew to Massachusetts, where I was living at the time, then called me and came by my house. He said, "Man, I just feel so bad. With all the admiration we have for you—I feel so bad that you refuse to work with me." He said it with no viciousness. None at all.

I said, "Well, it's simple. It's because of the fact that you write a song that becomes the number one best-selling hit, 'Buffalo Soldier,' and you didn't know those black Buffalo soldiers were sent west by the Pentagon to kill the buffalo to starve the Indians to death?"

He said, "I didn't know that."

After that, I agreed to open up for his concert and we remained close until he died.

Buffalo soldiers were black soldiers the U.S. government organized in the nineteenth century, right after slavery ended. You know the people they fought against half the time? American Indians. Now, think about that. Europeans and white Americans enslaved blacks. Slavery started in America over one hundred fifty years before America was a country. And after America became independent, slavery went on for eighty-nine *more* years. So, all together, slavery in America lasted almost two hundred fifty years. Then, when it was finally over, what's the first thing the government does with those free blacks? Organizes them so they can fight against the *other* group the government had been abusing and slaughtering since the beginning: Indians. How do you like that?

And the black soldiers went ahead and did it. The Indians called them "Buffalo Soldiers" because they had woolly hair like buffalos. The blacks and the Indians were just like two chickens in a cockfight. What they should have done was team up and peck their *real* enemy to death instead of one another.

But it wasn't the black soldiers' fault. Not really.

Because, look here: black folks are always being compared to Jews. "How come black folks can't get themselves together like Jews?" I'll tell you why. When your baby is six years old, does he act like you act when you're thirty-seven? No. You see how simple it is? So, we've had our so-called freedom for 150 years, and we're going to compare ourselves to people who have been liberated for 9,000 years. I say go back to the first 350 years after Jews were liberated. They acted the same way we do now, because *the slave mentality was still in their heads.* It's the same with us now. That slave mentality is still in our heads. That's why the white man frees us from slavery and then tells us to go kill some Indians, and we almost kill *ourselves* trying to do it.

Because we don't value ourselves. Look here: black folks are the only people on the planet who call our women "strong" but our cars "beautiful." Something's wrong with that. A white man tells me that if my woman doesn't look like his, she can't be beautiful. And I *believe* it. I may see something in her, but I don't call it "beautiful." I call it "strong." We don't value ourselves. And it's because we've still got that slave crap in our heads.

Now, fast-forward. All these cops out here shoot blacks in the head, but they don't mess with black folks' *cars.* You ever had a black man come up and tell you, "A white racist cop took out a night stick and started smashing my car?" No? Why? Because black folks tell cops what they can hurt and kill and what they'd better not touch, because of what *we* value. If a cop hears you call your car "beautiful" and your woman "strong," whom is he going to hurt and what's he going to leave alone?

That's what's going on. But you all walk around in the middle of this mess every day and still don't see it. I didn't always see it, either. I spent millions of dollars doing all kinds of research. That's why they can't stop me from saying anything I say, because they know they'll be in trouble if they do. And as far as the white man killing me, they've tried that; it doesn't work. I say, "You guys, come on." I'm in the phone book. Never had a bodyguard.

See, there's a universal God that says to black people, "Death is better! I made you, but you let these crackers send you to war and you think you have to go instead of thinking, 'Death is better'?"

Now, think about the hundreds of thousands of blacks they tried to enslave who jumped ship. They don't tell you about that. Jumped ship, man. "Before I'll be a slave, I'll be buried in my grave"—yeah. Black people today *say* that, and then go right back to work for white folks. And not just work for them—go out and kill for them. Buffalo soldiers fighting Indians, black soldiers going over to kill yellow people in Vietnam, brown people in Afghanistan and Iraq—and why?

It's because we don't know to value ourselves. We know how to make potato salad and do all kinds of other BS. We know how to dance. But we don't know there's something *inside* us.

Look here: In the civil rights movement, we took on the mightiest military force that ever existed in the history of the planet, the U.S. government. Martin Luther King Jr.—I was with him. Nobody ever heard him say anything trifling about white folks. He was just as meek and humble—and brought them to their *knees*, man. But we don't talk about that.

Because we don't value ourselves. We don't know what we can do, even though we've already *seen* it.

Bill Clinton

If I could talk to Bill Clinton, I would apologize to him on be-half of black folks. Hear me out, now. Black folks tricked him. "The first black president!" They went in that big old black pot and said, "Here, white boy, you're black." And then they went *back* in that black pot and said, "Here, Obama, you ain't black *enough*." What kind of foolish behavior is this? You sure don't hear the Ku Klux Klan telling Obama he's too white. I'd apologize to Bill Clinton, because black folks tricked him. They've got him so confused he set up his office around black folks in Harlem! (It only sped up gentrification and now most of the blacks have been displaced.)

When he was young, one of my sons came to me crying. He said, "Daddy, my brothers and sisters are laughing at me."

I said, "Why?"

He said, "I built me a castle, and I make like it's my house. Do you see anything wrong with that?"

I said, "How old are you, boy?"

He said, "Eight years old."

I said, "Ain't nothin' wrong with that—until you start using it as your address."

So, I'd tell Bill Clinton: there's nothing wrong with being black, as long as you're only playing. But when you try to use it as your address . . .

I've got some questions for Bill Clinton. Have you and your wife and daughter ever been standing on a street corner in New York and had a cab pass you by because you were "the black president?" Has Chelsea ever been pulled over by white police because her daddy's "the black president?" Mr. President, do you know what it feels like to be a black person, to be a congresswoman or a lieu-tenant governor or somebody with twelve doctorates, and be driving down the street and hear the police siren? You start squeezing that steering wheel tight, and they pass by you, and you thank God? (*Damn* thanking God—you didn't do anything wrong in the first place!) When you know what that feels like, then you're black. Until then . . .

That's what this is about.

Now, look at some things Bill Clinton did and ask yourself if this sounds like somebody who ought to be called the first black president. Black folks should have seen it coming back in 1992, but we didn't. He ran for president that year. He wanted to prove he was tough on crime. Like I said before, anytime you hear the phrase "tough on crime," substitute "blacks" for "crime," and you get what's really going on. Before the New Hampshire primary, Clinton flew to Arkansas to oversee an execution, because he was still the governor there. The black man they were executing was named Ricky Ray Rector. This is how pitiful Rector was: on the last day of his life, when they gave him his last meal, he asked if they could save his dessert for him until the next morning. Okay? That poor brotha had the mind of a child, but that didn't stop them from killing him, and when it was over, Clinton said, "No one can say I'm soft on crime."

But we hadn't seen anything yet. That fall, he was elected president, and his war on black folks really got started then. He scrapped Aid to Families with Dependent Children and replaced it with Temporary Assistance for Needy Families. The key word there is *temporary*, because suddenly there was a five-year lifetime limit on welfare and food stamps, and if you were ever caught with so much as an ounce of weed, you wouldn't get a dime. You also wouldn't get into public housing if you were caught holding or selling drugs. So, if you got locked up, you might as well have *stayed* locked up, because if you got out of prison and your only plan was to head home to the projects, you would be *homeless*. Not that there was much public housing left once Clinton got through. The money they had used to build projects? It went to building prisons instead. And which people do you think those prisons were for?

There's your first black president.

Al Sharpton, the Pope, and White Supremacy

Let me show you something about how white supremacy works.

Before I do, I've got to say a few things about Al Sharpton. Did you know that he is probably the most powerful black person in America? He had a TV show on a white network, MSNBC, five days a week—now it's just on Sundays—which meant that a black man was talking to millions of Americans every day. Every time there's a racial situation in New York City, and it looks like there's going to be trouble, they go get Al to cool things down. Say what you want about that brotha, he is an American original. Where does somebody like him come from?

He was born in Brooklyn in 1954. He preached a sermon when he was *four years old*, was ordained when he was ten. That little boy went on tour with *Mahalia Jackson*! When he wasn't but fifteen, in 1969, Jesse Jackson named him youth director of Operation Breadbasket, and at eighteen he was youth director of Shirley Chisholm's campaign.

The man could draw attention like nobody you ever saw; he was an attention *magnet*. And he used that magnetism to keep the focus on what was happening to black people. If something happened to black folks in New York City, there was Al. In 1986, when three black men were assaulted in Howard Beach, Queens, and one of them got killed when he was chased into the path of a car—there was Al, leading a march through Howard Beach, making sure everybody was aware of the case, until New York governor Mario Cuomo appointed a special prosecutor.

In 1989, when Yusef Hawkins, sixteen years old, got shot and killed in Bensonhurst, Brooklyn, there was Al, leading marches.

In the 1990s, when Gavin Cato and Amadou Diallo were killed, there was Al.

Some people didn't like the way Al did things, but he called attention to injustices that wouldn't have gotten as much notice otherwise. And in doing that, he became prominent nationally. He ran for the U.S. Senate from New York in 1992, and maybe he didn't win, but let me tell you, a lot of people voted for that dude. And now he's in front of millions of TV viewers. A lot of black folks have a problem with his hair style, but when something goes wrong he's the first called. He's a powerful man.

And he's a preacher. Now, wouldn't you think that if the pope came through New York City, Al would be one of the people he'd see? Think again.

When the pope came to New York, the only black place he went to was Harlem—and Al wasn't invited. And all those crackers, including the mayor, and all of the rest Al thought were friends—*they* went. (David Dinkins, the first black mayor of New York, wasn't invited, either.) The pope comes through in his popemobile, hugging all those little white sick children, but when he went to Africa a month later, he didn't touch a black child. So, who is this guy? I'll tell you who: the latest representative of white supremacy.

Donald Trump

If you ever saw Donald Trump's television shows, you saw that he was brilliant. So, how did he get so stupid all at once? Something else you've got to wonder: if I went to apply for a job collecting garbage, they would ask me to bring in my last year's tax returns. But Trump runs for president and he doesn't bring *his* in, and y'all tolerate it? And now he's won, and you can't see where this is going?

People have asked me what we do now that Trump is president. There's nothing *to* do. It's over. We're in decline now. The Romans, the Greeks, the Egyptians—all of those empires fell. It's our turn now. We didn't see what was happening, and now it's too late.

We want to believe that everything was all right until the 2016 election, but it's never been all right. Take the Electoral College. Most folks who vote don't know that whoever wins the popular vote doesn't necessarily win the election. Most people could vote for me or you—but if the voters are fool enough to do that, the government could bring out the military, and that would be the end of that. So, this is not a free, democratic society.

We think we're a democracy because reporters interview celebrities, or talk to an executive here or there, or do man-on-the-street interviews. How come nobody ever interviews *rich* people? How come nobody ever interviews Henry Ford's family? The Rockefeller family? The DuPont family? How come we don't hear about the money they give, and whom they give it to?

We know one thing: if Donald Trump were doing something the superpowerful didn't like, they'd shoot him, just like they did John F. Kennedy. Think about the time the Secret Service grabbed somebody because someone else yelled, "He's got a gun," and they whisked Kennedy off the stage—and then, later, they said, "We didn't find a gun." And we don't question that. Are you going to ask the government where the gun is that killed Kennedy? The people who are doing the shootings and killings are also in charge of investigating them, and we don't see anything wrong with that?

Here's where we are now: the superrich people own the networks. If you're a reporter for CBS, NBC, or ABC, you can turn a story in, and they can legitimately tell you, "Well, I don't know if we can go with that; we might get a lawsuit." And it's *been* like that for a long time. Walter Cronkite, the anchor of *CBS Evening News* from 1962 to 1981—they called him the most trusted man in America—interviewed President Lyndon Baines Johnson on five different days, Monday through Friday. The interviews were supposed to run later. So, someone called me and said, "CBS and Cronkite just interviewed LBJ. Can I get you a copy?" I said, "Hey, yeah. But just leave it somewhere where I can get it, so nobody thinks I stole it." Now, up until that point, I thought LBJ had had something to do with Kennedy's murder. That was because of what had happened at the 1960 Democratic National Convention. At the time, LBJ was the Senate majority leader, the most powerful man in Congress, maybe in all of Washington. He was drunk when he came out onstage at the time when they nominated him to be Kennedy's vice president. He said, "I have more power in one day in the position I'm in now than the president will have in four years." At one point he left the stage, but then Sam Rayburn, the Speaker of the House, whispered something in his ear, and LBJ came back to the stage and said, "I accept the nomination." So, I figured Rayburn had told LBJ something *then* about how Kennedy was going to be killed.

Now, watch this. When he was interviewed by Walter Cronkite, here's what LBJ said, which changed my whole view: he said he believed Kennedy's murder was a conspiracy, and he believed that Lee Harvey Oswald was part of it, but a small part. I said, "Wow, man. He's saying *that?*"

When the five-part interview ran, the part where LBJ said that he thought Kennedy's death had been a conspiracy was cut out. I saw Walter Cronkite about two weeks later, and I said, "Hey, man, what happened to the part that was cut?" He said, "Well, CBS overruled me." I said, "But you're the man people trust. My grandmother doesn't call CBS 'Uncle Walty.' She calls *you* 'Uncle Walty.'" That's where the trust breaks down, but people don't know it.

What does that tell you? There is no democracy here. No freedom of information. The only free people are the ones with enough money to control the information you get. And this has been going on all along, but we want to believe that it has just started happening.

If there's any God at all, and there is, and that God doesn't do something to punish America, then that God owes Sodom and Gomorrah a *serious* apology. Because with technology and other things we have, the U.S. government does things to make those thugs look like angels.

Let's look at America for a minute. We talk about the right to vote; the right to *elect* is not important if you don't also have the right to *select*. But who picks the candidates? It goes back to folks with money. But who gets blamed when things go wrong? *Us.*

For the 2016 election, they said, "Oh, black folks aren't coming out for the early vote." Right then they were fixing to blame things on us: "Oh, if black folks had come out, Hillary would have won." Well, when Obama beat Hillary, they blamed that on us, too—they said it was because of the black vote. Now, if you were alive and on this planet at the time, you know that a lot of black folks were supporting the Clintons. Bob Johnson, who owned BET, was talking about Obama's drug problems. But when Hillary lost to Trump, suddenly it was black folks' fault.

If I could, I would take all black folks to Germany and let them study the Jews. The difference between the Jews and what Hitler did to them, and us here and what's being done to us: the

Jews never thought they were part of Hitler's system. But we think we're part of the American system of government! There was no Jewish secretary of state under Hitler. Jews weren't going to fight in wars for Germany. But we fight for the United States. And to believe that we are part of the American system is like believing white people can cook chitlins better than black folks.

I am so sick and tired of seeing a black person shot in the back, shot dead, followed by people saying, "Not all cops are bad." You know how many lawyers get disbarred every year? But you never hear, "Not all lawyers are bad." You know how many doctors lose their medical licenses? But you never hear anybody talking about, "Not all doctors are bad." Police departments are *filthy*. If I pay a lawyer, I don't expect him to sue *me*. If I go to a doctor, he's not supposed to *give me* a disease. But we pay taxes so cops will protect us, and they shoot us instead—and the response is, "Not all cops are bad"? And still we think we're part of America.

America is *afraid*. That's why Trump was elected. You've got white families that would be in their fifth generation of sending their kids to Princeton, Yale, Harvard, Stanford, but they've got their kids in community college. You've got white families where the children have three or four PhDs but they're living in their parents' basements. Those families see something wrong. So that's what Trump tapped into. It's like if you and your child are hit by a car, and the ambulance driver is somebody you've seen on TV calling black folks "nigger," but you have no choice but to go with *him* to the hospital, thinking it makes any difference *what* you do. That's what *fear* does. It's the same fear that Trump exploited, and other Republicans exploited, to make us afraid of Islam.

Going into the 2016 election, we knew something big was planned. What happened, Trump's victory, was the action of a handful of thug pimp punks with money—not millions of fool voters. Not even the CIA or the FBI. There's something going on in this country that scares the people whose job it is to scare people. So, we need to be careful, because we don't know how big this is.

Ben Carson and the Operation to Separate the Binder Twins

Patrick and Benjamin Binder were twins, born in February 1987. They were joined at the head. The operation to un-join them took place at Johns Hopkins the following September. Dr. Ben Carson, now the U.S. secretary for Housing and Urban Development, gets the credit for separating them. But did he? If you paid attention during the 2016 campaign, you'd have thought he wasn't even in the room when that operation took place. Now, let's look at it. The whole time he campaigned for president, he never mentioned the operation. Everybody else mentioned what they did that's positive! If he did it, why didn't he talk about it?

Ralph Ellison, author of *Invisible Man*

The novel *Invisible Man* was published in 1952. It's about a young black man who has all kinds of adventures as he makes his way from the South to the North. Sold a whole mess of copies, won the National Book Award.

Black American "Ambassadors"

Black America becoming prominent around the world in the twentieth century really had to do with nonwhite people around the world. America had to show them something that would fit into their culture, because the only thing the United States was taking around the world was white supremacy, racism, and war. To make themselves look good, the government had to export something else. Let me give you an example.

The white folks in the U.S. government appropriated billions of dollars toward building things in Africa. Why? Because *there were natural resources there.* In fact, there's no place in Africa where the United States has built anything where there weren't natural resources involved. No place where they built schools or brought medicine where there weren't natural resources.

Now, to make it look good, the United States had to send over somebody who looked like people in Africa. It had to get some famous black ambassadors. Didn't matter if they had experience. So, they took Satchmo (Louis Armstrong) and made him an "ambassador of goodwill," so no black folks around the planet would think we didn't have black ambassadors. You see? That was part of the trick. They didn't send over black entertainers who had *attitudes,* so Satchmo, Pearl Bailey—*these* are folks people overseas were listening to, so they didn't see anything wrong with America. You cannot read anything negative that Satchmo or Pearl Bailey said about this country.

They also sent black athletes who white people had heard of. They sent Mal Whitfield as an ambassador of goodwill but he ended up being the ambassador to five African countries. That's where they messed up. After Whitfield went there, that's when the East African runners started winning all of the long distance races around the world. Thank you, Mal.

The Deaths of Otis Redding and Sam Cooke

The singer Otis Redding, a week before his plane crashed, was stupid enough to have a press conference and say, "Jews will not control

black music anymore. Two weeks from now, we'll have a company."
And the next week, his plane went down. Same thing with the
singer Sam Cooke, when he got shot at that motel in Los Angeles
by the motel's female manager, after he supposedly tried to rape a
woman there. Whatever happened, Sam was doing the same thing
Otis was doing: talking about controlling black music. Instead of
focusing on that, the media give you a scandal, and everybody buys
into that; that's all they can talk about: "Ooooh, he was trying to
rape somebody and got shot."

Jesus

I go all over the world. I go to China and check out the Christian
communities there. In paintings of Jesus, he looks Chinese. When
I go to India, the pictures of Jesus make him look Indian. I go to
Brazil, Jesus looks Brazilian. I come back home to America, go in
the black community, into black churches, and Jesus is a white man.
And you wonder what's wrong with your children and why they
don't love themselves? That's that slave mentality again.

Christ was born in a place where there were nothing *but* black
people, and when he picked his disciples, he picked not only eleven
Europeans, but eleven *Englishman?* Peter, Paul, Matthew—where
do names like that come from where Jesus was born? All twelve of
them were white boys except the one who killed Christ—he's an
Arab Jew: Judas.

Condoleezza Rice

Condoleezza Rice had more PhDs than the president's whole Cab-
inet, but they called her "Condie." And black people didn't even see
anything wrong with it. They didn't call Madeleine Albright "Mad-

die"! Bill Clinton's attorney general, Janet Reno—did they call her "Jannie"? Hell, no. But it didn't bother Condoleezza Rice. See how we've been programmed?

Evolution and Revolution

See, revolution is the extension of evolution. Evolution is a gradual and mysterious change that leads to revolution, which is quick change. When a woman gets pregnant, the first nine months of pregnancy is evolution. When her water breaks, that's revolution—quick change.

It's time to change the world.

4

Making Something Out of Nothing

My grandmother doesn't have space in her head to believe there could be a Baptist on Mars.

When my wife, Lil, and I first got together, I said, "If you want this to work—because I don't give a damn—it's not about love; it's about can you be lovable?" And I guess she heard me. We've been married fifty-eight years. That's lovability, not love! Love's associated with being evil when you think somebody else is looking at your woman; being lovable is not. But we take the wrong idea from messed-up love songs.

The Blues

The worst music I ever heard that promotes violence, greed, and misogyny wasn't hip-hop; it was black blues. We're the only group of men on planet Earth who sing derogatory words about our women. "I caught my baby in bed with my best friend—one two, three, four, gimme some more, shake your money maker"— anytime anybody says "Shake your money maker," they're talking about your vagina. When you make money with it, you're a ho. Men and women dance to this kind of thing. Listen to hillbilly music, and see if they ever sing anything derogatory about the women they're living in their trailers with. All they say is, "Baby, I'm sor-ry."

Yet, nobody complains about the blues. When I was growing up, people took pride in the blues. I listened to that crap, and I thought, "I'm a black man, and between me and this black woman, I'm the trifling one." But our songs don't reflect that.

In St. Louis, when I was growing up, nobody came there but blues singers. Where were you going to see another kind of entertainer? I try to avoid listening to the blues. Ever listen to the blues and wonder why your love affairs are so bad? "My baby done lef' me"—little five-year-old children singing that mess. "My baby done lef' me." That's why I used to slip off to the opera, man. I didn't want to hear none of that blues mess. A bluesman will sing about blue Monday. Man, you're going to take the universal God's Monday and make it blue because *you* messed up? Blue Monday! Ain't that a bitch, huh?

What I'm saying is be careful with what you let into your mind. I don't know anyone who loves the blues who is happy. The arts and creative endeavors are serious business.

The Harlem Renaissance

The first two decades of the twentieth century were a crucial time for black folks.

I already told you about black people running from the South like it was on fire, going north and west to try to find better jobs and get out from under the thumb of the Ku Klux Klan, convict leasing, and all that other racist mess.

Then came World War I. Now, President Woodrow Wilson was a segregationist, but that didn't stop him from talking about democracy until his lips were about to fall off. When he got the United States involved in the war against Germany in 1917, he said it was "to make the world safe for democracy." Blacks folks were a big part of that. Three hundred sixty-seven thousand black people joined the armed forces in World War I, and two hundred thousand went to fight in Europe. This wasn't like the Civil War, when black men were fighting not to be slaves. Over in Europe, we were fighting for our country and for the world. We fought bravely, and a lot of us didn't come back. Then, after going over there and fighting and dying for democracy and for the sake of the world, black men came back here wanting some democracy of our *own*, but guess what we found instead? The same old racist crap. Segregation, job discrimination, housing discrimination (and every other kind of -ation you could think of), here in our *home* nation, everything we had faced before, in the North and South—only, now we weren't having it. We protested, and when whites tried to get violent, black people got violent *back*.

Up north, in the cities, black folks got what you'd call *consciousness*. We started thinking about our situation and decided that we weren't going to get pushed around like before. We also found a lot of ways to express what we were feeling—about race and politics, but also about *life*. And that's how the Harlem Renaissance was born. There were so many black people in Harlem, in New York City, that it was like the capital of black America. That's why so many black novelists, poets, painters, and musicians made their way to Harlem. It was a black artistic explosion. (It was a long time before I knew anything about it. Where were you going to learn it in St. Louis, where I grew up?)

The Harlem Renaissance was something, man. So many great artists. Writers like Langston Hughes, Zora Neale Hurston, Claude McKay, Countee Cullen, Jessie Redmon Fauset, Rudolph Fisher, Jean Toomer, Arna Bontemps, and James Weldon Johnson. Painters and sculptors such as William H. Johnson, Malvin Gray Johnson, Archibald J. Motley Jr., Aaron Douglas, Augusta Savage, and Jacob Lawrence. There were even movie directors, like Oscar Micheaux, whose brother ran a bookstore in Harlem where a lot of intellectual black folks hung out, talking about the issues of the day. If you want to talk about music, that was the period when Louis Armstrong, Duke Ellington, Sidney Bechet, Eubie Blake, and a whole bunch more came into their own—and sooner or later, all of them found their way to Harlem.

In some respects, the Harlem Renaissance was similar to other movements: by the time somebody got around to giving it a name, it was already going strong. That was true of jazz and the blues, too. But if you want to point to an official starting date for the Harlem Renaissance, you'd have to mention Alain LeRoy Locke.

Alain Locke was born in Philadelphia in 1885. He went to Harvard University and became the first black Rhodes Scholar, studying over in England. Then he started teaching at Harvard, where W. E. B. Du Bois encouraged him to get his PhD. In 1918, Locke wrote an essay called "The Role of the Talented Tenth." Just like W.E.B., he thought it was the duty of college-educated blacks to lead other black folks. In 1925, he put together a special Harlem issue of a magazine called *Survey Graphic*, and that same year, he edited a whole book called *The New Negro*. Man, what *didn't* that book have in it? All kinds of work by black folks—writing by Toomer, McKay, Bontemps, Hurston, Fisher, James

Weldon Johnson, Du Bois, Kelly Miller, E. Franklin Frazier, and a whole bunch of others; artwork by Aaron Douglas and Miguel Covarrubias.

Locke writes near the end of the introduction to the book, "Negro life is not only establishing new contacts and founding new centers, it is finding a new soul. There is a fresh spiritual and cultural focusing. . . . There is a renewed race-spirit that consciously and proudly sets itself apart." It was on.

So much great work. Jacob Lawrence made a whole bunch of paintings about what's called the Great Migration from the South. The paintings are powerful; you could look at them all day. You've heard about Sherlock Holmes and Watson? One was a detective; the other was a doctor? Well, the Harlem Renaissance writer Rudolph Fisher wrote about a character who was a doctor *and* a detective, and the book was sharp as hell. Check it out: *The Conjure-Man Dies.* Or another novel he wrote: *The Walls of Jericho.* Those black folks had a sense of humor, too. George S. Schuyler wrote a novel called *Black No More*, about a dude who came up with a way to turn black people white.

None of them topped Langston Hughes, though. He captured the spirit of the whole thing. He'd write poems that were beautiful but seemed simple and easy to write—till you tried to do it yourself, that is. Take his poem "Harlem Night Song." Look at this here:

Across
The Harlem roof-tops
Moon is shining.
Night sky is blue.
Stars are great drops
Of golden dew.

And this:

Come,
Let us roam the night together
Singing.

George Washington Carver

George Washington Carver was a brilliant scientist. But what do you know about him? Right—he came up with all kinds of stuff to do with the peanut. That makes people laugh, and it makes him sound like a joke, when Carver was one of the most brilliant people this country ever produced. He helped a whole lot of folks. Some of the ways he helped southern farmers involved peanuts and some didn't.

Carver was born into slavery in Missouri in the 1860s. A white German dude named Moses Carver had bought George's parents in the 1850s. George's father died before George was born, and most of George's eleven brothers and sisters died before they were grown. In the years when George was a baby, kidnappers would come from Arkansas at night and snatch blacks folks, slaves and free blacks alike, and sell them into slavery. They grabbed George and his mother when George wasn't but a week old. There are a couple of stories about how George got rescued. As one story goes, when the kidnappers were riding away, George fell off the buckboard of the wagon and some kind folks found him and took him to a home for lost children until his owner came and got him. Another: George's master paid a detective to find the kidnapped kids. In any case, they never found George's mother, but George and his brother made it back to Moses Carver, and after slavery ended, Moses raised them as his own kids. That shows you something right there. Moses Carver was from Germany—he wasn't raised with the same kind of racist BS as folks in America. It didn't stop him from owning slaves, but it *did* mean that when slavery was over, he was willing to treat George like his own. And Moses's wife must have felt the same way, because she taught George to read and write.

Where George grew up, though, most white folks *didn't* feel that way, and because he was black, he wasn't allowed to attend public school. There was a school for blacks ten miles away, though, in Neosho, Missouri, right near the Kansas border, and George wanted to learn so bad that he lived with a family in Fort Scott, Kansas, in order to attend. But he left Fort Scott after he saw some white folks kill a black man right in front of him—he never forgot that. He went to a bunch of different schools before he graduated from high school in Kansas. After that, he worked as a farmer and a ranch hand before going back to school at Simpson College, in Iowa. One of his instructors noticed how well George could paint flowers and plants—he painted all his life—and suggested that he study botany at Iowa State Agricultural College, and that's where he headed next. He was the school's first black student. He got a bachelor's and a master's degree there, and he wrote a thesis about plants engineered by humans.

You've already read about Booker T. Washington running the Tuskegee Institute. Well, he brought George Washington Carver to Tuskegee in 1896 to run the Agriculture Department. Carver stayed for forty-seven years.

Now, here's where the BS comes in. When people talk about Carver's work, usually during Black History Month, they'll say, "Oh, yeah, that's that dude who thought of all the ways you can use a peanut," which makes you picture a grown-ass man sitting there playing with peanuts all day. Yes, George did invent products made from peanuts, but the truth is most of them didn't sell. What he *did* do was he saw that soil was worn out because farmers kept planting cotton all the time. He said that if it was going to grow anything anymore, and if farmers and other folks wanted to make money, not to mention eat, the soil had to be restored. So, he came up with the idea to get nitrogen back into the soil through what is now called crop rotation: in between planting cotton, farmers could plant sweet potatoes, soybeans, and, yes, peanuts. George Washington Carver saved southern farmers, which is the same thing as saying he saved the South.

A black man saved the South. Think about that for a minute.

Carver was tight with Henry Ford, the automaker. Ford knew how brilliant Carver was. Ford had a plantation in Georgia, and Carver helped oversee the crops there. In exchange, Ford donated a lot of money to the Tuskegee Institute. Later, during World War II, when Ford needed rubber for his cars but there was a shortage because the military needed it for weapons, Ford and Carver worked together with different plants until they discovered that goldenrod could be used to make a rubber substitute.

Now, let me take you up to the universal level. Here's how the universe works. That Ford boy didn't *invent* the car. The automobile was invented by the Duryea brothers in Massachusetts. Ford and the other automakers stole it. What did Ford invent? The plant! In other words, before that, you made cars one at a time. Then Ford came up with the assembly line. With it, they could make a whole bunch of cars at once.

How did that happen? One day, George Washington Carver said to Henry Ford, "I've got a package for you to take back to show your engineers. This is the study of plants. If they study this, and see the way plants work, you can make more than one car at a time." That's why the site of mass production for products all over the world is called a "plant."

Louis Armstrong

Talking about the Harlem Renaissance, I mentioned Louis Armstrong. Trumpet player. Singer. Born in New Orleans in 1901. Died seventy years later. In those seventy years, he turned American music on its head.

Around the time Armstrong was born, his daddy left him and his mama. Louis was born in a part of New Orleans called Back o' Town. Now, that should tell you something right there. Poor? That little boy had to scrape around in garbage cans just to find something to eat. Where he grew up was full of prostitutes, so that little rag-wearing somebody grew up fast. One thing they had there: dance halls. So, Louis Armstrong grew up hearing the blues and this other kind of music that was so new it didn't even have an official name yet. Armstrong was around ten years old when a newspaper first called it "jazz."

Like a lot of poor kids, Armstrong had a way of getting into trouble, and one time it got so bad that they put him in a home. And that's where somebody put a cornet—like a trumpet, but smaller—in the boy's hand. Nothing was the same after that, for him or for us.

He learned to play, and when he got a little older, he performed in a jazz band with a dude named King Oliver. Later he formed his own band, called the Hot Five; another band of his was called the Hot Seven. You want to talk about some trumpet playing? He made that thing sound like a bull charging around, like something was coming at you, and if you didn't get out the way, you'd be sorry. They say Armstrong played so loud that when he recorded with his band, he had to stand outside the room with the door open just so he wouldn't drown everybody else out. Those tunes he recorded in the 1920s, like "West End Blues," "Potato Head Blues," and "Wild Man Blues"—they still sound fresh today, like he's got something to say and he's saying it through his horn.

But it wasn't just that he played a ferocious trumpet. Beginning with Armstrong, musicians could play as *individuals*. The sound didn't have to be from the whole band; it could be your own expression, too.

Armstrong got the nicknames "Pops" and "Satchmo." They called him that second one because his mouth was so big it looked like an open satchel bag—"satchel mouth" became "Satchmo." Whatever they called him, he revolutionized playing—singing, too. His voice had that scratchy sound; when you heard him, you knew in a second who it was. After that, folks didn't want to hear singing with fancy European airs and all the rest of that prissy stuff. Pops taught America what singing was all about.

Duke Ellington

There's a whole lot of things folks can't agree on. But here's one thing *everybody* agrees on, whether they're black or white, rich or poor: life isn't fair. You ask a rich man why he gets to inherit all that money and have all those cars and women when other folks don't have a pot to piss in, and he'll shrug and tell you, "Hey, don't blame me. Life isn't fair." A poor man trying to explain to his woman why he can't afford to give her diamonds and bracelets and fancy vacations the way other men do for their women—he'll tell her, "Ain't my fault. I'm out here busting my behind like everybody else. But life isn't fair."

To *prove* it isn't fair, check this out: a hundred people had to go without good looks, brains, charm, and every last bit of natural talent just so one black man born in 1899 could have it all: Mr. Edward Kennedy Ellington. That's Duke Ellington to you.

Duke was born in Washington, DC, and made his way as a

young man to New York City and Harlem. Up there, money was
tight at first, but he got by, playing piano at rent parties (which
were just what they sound like: parties folks held to raise money
to pay the rent). Some of the other black dudes playing at those
parties were the best piano men around: James P. Johnson, Fats
Waller, Willie "the Lion" Smith. They called Smith "the Lion" because of his bravery in France in World War I. See there? Anywhere you go, there's a black person kicking ass. Johnson, Waller,
and Smith played what was called stride piano. Think about your
favorite basketball player running up and down the court like he
owns it, and that's what those three men did on piano. They could
make the keys do *anything*—little bit of classical technique, whole
lot of black style. Now, Duke couldn't play better than those men;
maybe he couldn't even play as well as them. But you'd better believe he learned from them.

Then he took that knowledge and mixed it up with everything
else: his brains, his good looks and fancy clothes, his smooth talk, his
style and charm. That man could charm the wings off a bumblebee.
That was one black man who didn't let racism touch him. He just
glided *past* it to get where he was going, like Michael Jordan going in
for a layup. It was like he charmed racism itself. He could also turn
that smooth charm on anybody. Duke had women like a library's got
books. He had other kinds of appetites, too. He could eat hot dogs
and ice cream like nobody you ever saw, without getting fat, and he
could drink you under the table. Duke was so smooth that he could
fire you from his band without your even realizing it. He wouldn't
say, "You're fired." He'd just hire somebody else who played the same
instrument as you, only thirteen times better, to the point where you
were so embarrassed you'd up and fire your*self*.

He even stole other band leaders' players that same smooth way.
Ben Webster, a tenor sax player, was playing in Cab Calloway's

band but wanted to play with Duke. And Duke wanted Ben. He told him, "I would love to have you in the band, but Cab is my brother and I can't take anybody out of his band. But if you didn't have a job, I'd have to give you one." Next thing you know, Ben had quit Cab's band. Since he wasn't with Cab anymore, Duke hired him. See how smooth he was?

If Duke met folks he *couldn't* charm, he was ready for them, too. His road manager said that Duke packed a pistol and knew how to use it.

Duke had his own way of doing things. Seven or eight decades before folks started talking about "thinking outside the box," one of his favorite sayings was "No boxes." Short and to the point, right? He was like that with music, too: any idea you could think of, he had already done it, and done it better.

Here's one idea Duke had: When he started leading bands and composing music for them, he used his imagination, but he observed what was going on around him, too. He said, "You can't write music right unless you know how the man that'll play it plays poker. You've got to write with certain men in mind. You write just for their abilities and natural tendencies and give them places where they do their best." He did that for just about all his band members. And they became famous for it, all over the world.

He wrote music that way for Johnny Hodges, who played the alto saxophone. Hodges had that sweet sound—he could play one note so nice you'd forget there *were* other notes.

He wrote music that way for Harry Carney, who played this low sound on the baritone sax and gave Duke's tunes the growl they had sometimes.

He wrote music that way for Cat Anderson and Cootie Williams, who played trumpet notes so high you felt like you were hearing something from outer space.

Duke wrote music that way for his whole big band—sweet-playing Johnny Hodges, growling Harry Carney, screaming trumpets, creamy woodwinds, and rumbling bass—and he didn't forget to put those drums in there. And the whole time, Duke himself would be tinkling those piano keys and signaling the band with his eyes. That was one smoking hot band.

It was even hotter after Duke hooked up with Billy Strayhorn and started recording some of the tunes that *that* little five-foot-three-inch, glasses-wearing dude wrote: "Lush Life," "Chelsea Bridge," "Take the 'A' Train."

The Duke Ellington Orchestra was an *international* band. It wasn't just that they went everywhere—oh, Duke traveled to more countries than a lot of folks have *heard* of, met presidents and prime ministers, kings and queens—but what made them an *international* band was they could go anywhere, and hear the music there, and Duke would write music inspired by that country, and he could make the music sound like it came both from that country *and* from a black, fried chicken–eating brother from DC. Which it was. That's why he could make albums and call 'em *Far East Suite* and *The Afro-Eurasian Eclipse*. (Go listen to *Far East Suite* and check out a tune called "Blue Pepper," and see if you can keep your feet from moving. I dare you.) He didn't forget about the folks back home—one of his best records was called *Harlem*, and another was called *New Orleans Suite*—but Duke was at home anywhere in the world.

Hattie McDaniel's Oscar for *Gone with the Wind*

In 1936, a white lady named Margaret Mitchell published a novel called *Gone with the Wind*. It had more pages than ten phone books. The novel was set in the South during the Civil War. The Civil War lasted from 1861 to 1865—four years. That's about how long it would take you to read *Gone with the Wind*, not including the time you'd spend either falling asleep or stomping your feet and hollering over that racist BS.

In 1939, they released the movie version of *Gone with the Wind*. Folks flocked to see that piece of crap. It set all kinds of box-office records and won just about every award Hollywood had to give out. Among other things, it was the first time a movie character said the word *damn* on-screen. That's what I said when I saw it: *Damn*.

Another thing the movie is known for: Hattie McDaniel, who plays a house slave, became the first black person to win an Academy Award. Her character is named Mammy. Black folks gave her a hard time for playing a black stereotype. Then, when she was doing an interview and they asked her how she felt about always playing a maid, even with all her talent, here's what she said in response: "I'd rather play a maid than be one." With that statement, she insulted black domestic workers.

Well, one day, I stood in line to meet her. When I got to her, she was smiling. I told her, "You won't be smiling when you hear what I've got to say to you. Ninety-eight percent of black women were maids. They ain't never did no drugs, they ain't never laid down and screwed white boys—they might have if they had the chance, but they didn't. That was my *mama* you were talking about." I couldn't be too hard on her, though, because she helped open the door for black actors.

Marian Anderson Sings on the Steps of the Lincoln Memorial

Marian Anderson had a dignity about her that a lot of people didn't associate with black folks. She was a great singer, but it wasn't even her singing that got all the attention. Hell, we'd heard high notes in church like the ones she hit. What made her so famous was what happened in Washington, DC, in 1939. The world was watching then.

She was born in Philadelphia in 1897. Her daddy sold coal and ice at the train station, and her mama had taught school in Virginia, even though she didn't have a degree. Up in Philly, white women with no degree could teach school, but not black ones, so she ended up working as a cleaning woman and taking in folks' laundry. The family went to a Baptist church. Marian Anderson's aunt liked her singing and told her she ought to join the choir, which she did, at age six. Anderson always gave her aunt credit for her becoming a singer.

After she finished high school, Marian applied to the Philadelphia Academy of Music. They told her flat out, "We don't take colored." But she took private lessons, and in 1925 she won the top prize in a contest that the New York Philharmonic put on. After that, she started singing around the country—well, as much as she could; a lot of places didn't want a black woman singing.

After a while, Anderson had had enough of that crap, so she went to Europe, where she got treated better. Jean Sibelius, a famous Finnish composer, heard Anderson sing and was so impressed that he asked her over to his place and wined and dined her. He even started writing music for her. She was getting treated the way she *should* have been treated back home.

Anderson soon built up a big following, but even *that* didn't make a difference to racists back in her home country. She'd land singing gigs in different places in the States, then get there only to learn that the hotel she wanted to stay in or the restaurant where she wanted to eat wasn't going to let her in. That's how deep race hatred ran: she was a famous singer, but she wasn't good enough to pay to sleep in their beds or eat their food.

You know where she was allowed to sleep once, though? She went to sing at Princeton University and couldn't get a room, but Albert Einstein let her stay at his house. Einstein was the smartest man the world had ever seen, and he was against racial prejudice.

Then came the incident that got everybody's attention. In 1939, the Daughters of the American Revolution wouldn't let Anderson sing in front of a mixed-race audience at Constitution Hall, in Washington, DC. Now, to give them credit, a whole bunch of the DAR's members quit over that. One of them was the First Lady at the time, Eleanor Roosevelt. She and the president helped arrange it so that Anderson could sing outside, on the steps of the Lincoln Memorial. Seventy-five thousand people attended the outstanding performance.

The damage was already done to America's reputation, though. Reporters from around the world swooped in to write about how America, the Land of the Free, wasn't free enough to let a black woman sing in a concert hall.

To tell the truth, that's how a lot of race progress has been made in America. The country gets shamed into doing things it doesn't want to do.

Charlie Parker

Ever heard the saying "cruel to be kind"? The jazz alto sax player Charlie Parker—they called him "Bird"—found out how true that is. Bird came from two Kansas Cities: born in the one in Kansas in 1920, raised in the one in Missouri. In that second one, he worked hard to be a jazz musician. As a teenager, he bit off more than he could chew—one time, anyway. He took his saxophone on the bandstand with some older musicians. One of them was the drummer Papa Jo Jones. Papa Jo didn't mess around. If you got on the stand with him, you'd better know what you were doing, or he'd let you know right quick. Bird was no exception. He started playing with Papa Jo and couldn't keep up, and finally Papa took one of his big old shiny cymbals off his drum kit and threw it—some say he threw it at the middle of the stage; some say he threw it at Bird's head. Either way, it landed with a crash so loud they probably heard it back in the other Kansas City. And when it landed, Bird wasn't sleeping, but that crash woke him up.

That's what I'm saying about "cruel to be kind." What Papa Jo did was cruel, but he did Bird a favor. Because, after that, Bird saw what he had to do. He started practicing that horn like nobody you ever saw. After a while, nobody could touch him. He played like he had rockets at the ends of his fingers. He soon became known around Kansas City, Missouri, in Jay McShann's band.

Then, in 1939, he moved to New York City, and that's where he really made his contribution. He met Dizzy Gillespie, the trumpeter, who could play as fast as Bird could, and the two of them and some others played all night in clubs in Harlem, and that's where bebop was born. Back then, the clubs had what they called cutting contests, with each musician trying to top the others, playing fast to keep out the chumps. But not just by playing fast: you'd be playing and struggling to keep up, and maybe you *almost* could, and then they'd change the key of the song, and suddenly you were eating some dust.

Here's a story about Bird that's in a couple of books. This is how much Bird knew about music—not just jazz, but *all* music, including classical. This is what a genius he was. One night, he was playing in a club and Igor Stravinsky walked in. Stravinsky was Russian, one of the most important classical music composers of the time; he was to twentieth-century classical music what Bird was to jazz, and that's saying something. Anyway, Bird was playing, and his trumpeter, Red Rodney, whispered in his ear that

Stravinsky had just sat down in the audience. Bird didn't even look at Stravinsky. But then, in the solo he was playing, he worked in a little bit of Stravinsky's music, from *The Firebird Suite*. He fit that music into what he was already playing like you'd fit a bolt onto a nut. Stravinsky laughed so hard he pounded his tabletop and his drink splashed on people nearby.

Bird was a wild man, loved to clown. He liked to throw around fancy words to be funny, like calling Dizzy Gillespie "my worthy constituent," and while you were still figuring out what he'd said, he'd start playing some of his lightning-fast, out-of-this-world music, and then you'd have to figure *that* stuff out. Now, racist whites like to say Martin Luther King Jr. was a Communist, but if anybody was a Communist, it was Bird, because he treated money like it belonged to everybody. He'd cheat the members of the bands he led and keep the money, but then he'd give you every cent out of his pocket if you needed it.

Like a lot of geniuses (like most folks, in fact), Bird had some bad habits—except Bird's habits weren't just bad; they were deadly. When he wasn't playing music, he was shooting heroin, and when he wasn't doing either of those, he was drinking. That stuff took its toll. After he died at the home of his friend the Baroness Pannonica de Koenigswarter, the coroner said he was around sixty years old—when Bird wasn't but thirty-four!

He did a lot with those thirty-four years, though. And just like Bird's *knowledge of* music went beyond jazz, his *impact on* music went beyond jazz, too. The jazz saxman John Coltrane—now *that* was a bad dude—what he did came out of what Bird did, and "Trane" influenced all kinds of musicians. Trane played fast and hard—you never saw a dude that intense—and he had this drummer, Elvin Jones, who used to play so hard he'd make Trane play that much faster and harder.

But it wasn't just other jazz musicians digging that stuff. John Densmore, the white drummer for the Doors, one of the biggest rock groups of all time, said he used to check out how Elvin Jones drove Trane, and that made Densmore drive the Doors' lead singer, Jim Morrison. And you can trace that all the way back to Bird. That's why, in so many cases, if you're talking about American culture, you're really talking about black culture.

But back to Bird: he left behind a whole lot of two-and three-minute records: "Ornithology," "Yardbird Suite," "Cool Blues," "Relaxin' at Camarillo"—he named that one for the mental hospital where he had to chill out for a while—"Scrapple from the Apple," "Klact-oveeseds-tene," "Parker's Mood," and a whole bunch more. They *needed* to be only two or three minutes long because they had more notes in them than most songs—that's how fast Parker and the rest of those dudes could play. Fast, and dazzling—but sometimes those songs were moving, too. Bird had speed *and* soul.

Miles Davis, Billie Holiday, Nina Simone, and Real Defiance

Miles Davis, jazz trumpeter, composer, band leader—he was a smooth, tough motherfucker. He didn't talk much. He let his music speak for him. Off the bandstand, he didn't make a lot of noise, but you didn't want to mess with him. On the stand, he played some of the most beautiful music you ever heard in your life, music that seemed to have in it all the pain and mournfulness and hope that black folks ever felt. That shows you black people at our best: fierce when we have to be, creating beauty when we have the chance.

That movie they just made about Miles was BS. They made up that stuff about the guns and the car chase because they think black people and violence go together like red beans and rice. And

Don Cheadle, who directed the movie and played Miles—he *admitted* that to get the movie financed, they had to put a white co-star in it. That shows you what we're dealing with. Miles would have not been pleased. He understood racism at its highest level like most dark skin men do. He was the first musician to have a black woman on an album cover. Imagine if black folks had all the power, and white folks wanted to make a movie about Thomas Jefferson writing the Declaration of Independence, but to get it made, they had to put a made-up black man in there, looking over Jefferson's shoulder while he was writing and saying, "Okay . . . all right . . . 'life, liberty,' yeah, good . . . you makin' me proud, Tom . . . don't forget 'pursuit of happiness.'" What do you think white folks would say? It would be five words. Would the words be "a beautiful celebration of diversity," or would they be "What's that nigger doing there?" You get only one guess.

That film didn't tell you anything about what Miles did—like being part of the bebop revolution with Charlie Parker, Dizzy Gillespie, and Thelonious Monk, playing music so hip and fast and complex that people are *still* in awe of what they did, with tunes like "Donna Lee" and "Be-Bop." Like inventing the "cool" style of jazz in the 1950s with the record *Birth of the Cool*. Like giving the world *Kind of Blue*, the best-selling jazz album of all time and one of the most beautiful records ever made by anybody, anywhere. Like spearheading jazz-rock fusion in the late 1960s with *Bitches Brew*. And all through it, Miles was smooth and hard as black glass.

Here's one thing, though. People talk about how "defiant" Miles was because when he was on the bandstand, he'd turn his back on the people who'd paid to see him. Man, when jazz musicians start playing their solos, they get so deep into them they close their eyes—Miles might have turned his back on the crowd because he forgot where they were *at!*

Anyway, if you want to talk about some black musicians being defiant, let's talk about two women: Billie Holiday and Nina Simone.

Billie Holiday—she was different from Ella Fitzgerald, who was singing at the same time. Ella had that *range*; she'd hit notes up past where you couldn't see without a telescope. Listen to Ella, you think, "Man, let me just sit back and enjoy this, 'cause ain't no way *I* could do it." But Billie had that easy, lazy sound to her voice that almost made you think you could sing just as well as her—till you tried it! That was her secret weapon: she made it sound so easy to do. She teamed up with Lester Young on saxophone—she'd sing, and he'd play, wearing that porkpie hat and holding that sax sideways—and listening to them play together was like hearing the sound of love and affection. Billie was the one who nicknamed him "Prez," for "president."

But my point about Billie Holiday is she recorded that song "Strange Fruit" about lynching. That was in 1939. Back then, in some parts of the country, if you were a black man, you could find yourself on a chain gang for not getting out of the way of a white person on the sidewalk. That's what was going on when Billie sang these words: "Southern trees bear strange fruit / blood on the leaves and blood at the root / black bodies swingin' in the southern breeze / strange fruit hangin' from the poplar trees." Now *that's* real defiance.

Then you had Nina Simone. Now *that* lady had some talent. Number six out of eight children in a family that was *subpoor*—you hear me? They would've had to borrow some money just to have *no* money. But Nina started playing piano at age three and had so much talent that she studied classical piano at Juilliard. Those folks don't let in just anybody, and if you want to know what an understatement is, that there is an understatement. But all that classical training didn't knock the feeling and *soul* out of her voice. You want to hear some feeling, you want to feel something yourself, listen to her sing "Feeling Good." And if you want to know what scat singing is all about, listen to what she does at the end of that song.

But my point about *her* is that in 1964 she recorded "Mississippi Goddam," which is one hell of a song. While black folks were having fire hoses and dogs trained on them, Nina sang:

Picket lines, school boycotts
They try to say it's a Communist plot
All I want is equality
for my sister my brother my people and me . . .

You don't have to live next to me
Just give me my equality.

That's defiance, too. Miles may have turned his back on his audience, but Nina didn't turn her back on her people. Billie, neither. Goddam.

Jackie Wilson

You can't always look at what a person is doing *now* and know what he *might* do. The singer Jackie Wilson proved that.

He was born in 1934 in Detroit. He started singing at an early age because he went to church with his mama and heard the singing there, but he started doing some other things early, too, like drinking wine and getting into trouble. The dude wasn't but nine when he started drinking. When he was a teenager, they sent him twice to a juvenile facility. He learned to box in there—well, he *boxed*; hard to say if he ever *learned* to box when his Golden Gloves record was 2 and 8! Maybe he couldn't fight too well, but he sure knew how to do some other things: he kept getting girls pregnant until the daddy of one of the girls made him marry her, and Jackie wasn't but seventeen. Now, all that might not make you think here's somebody who's going to leave his mark on the world. But he was, and he did.

Maybe he wasn't exactly Floyd Mayweather, and Jackie sure didn't know a thing about birth control, but when he got going on his solo singing career, that dude was *smooth*. They called him "Mr. Excitement." As a performer, he influenced Elvis Presley, James Brown, and Michael Jackson. Here's what I mean by smooth: James Brown would sing, and when he started to dance, you'd think, "Well, here's James dancing now." But Jackie Wilson was so smooth, doing it all at once, that you were almost too busy listening to that nice tenor voice to see what he was doing with his *body*; so smooth he made that stuff look easy. He'd get going on "Lonely Teardrops" or "Baby Workout," dressed like somebody going to a business meeting, and he'd hit those high notes like it was no big deal, so you almost didn't notice what his feet were doing.

Lorraine Hansberry and *A Raisin in the Sun*

The Great Migration is when black folks left the South and moved north and west, to places like New York, Philadelphia, Los Angeles, and Chicago. In most of the places we went to, we got packed into segregated neighborhoods like pants in a suitcase. Landlords knew we couldn't go anywhere else, so they charged us an arm and both legs for places that should have been condemned, that weren't fit for people to live in. Hell, even the rats and roaches were protesting.

One of Langston Hughes's poems, "Harlem," goes like this:

What happens to a dream deferred?
Does it dry up
like a raisin in the sun?
Or fester like a sore—
And then run?
Does it stink like rotten meat?
Or crust and sugar over—
like a syrupy sweet?

Maybe it just sags
like a heavy load.

Or does it explode?

"A dream deferred"—Hughes was talking about what happens to black folks when our dreams are not allowed to come to fruition because the dreamers are black.

What's the poem got to do with black folks moving from the South?

Lorraine Hansberry used a line from that poem, "a raisin in the sun," as the title of her play about a black family all bunched up together in a run-down Chicago apartment a few years after World War II. Three generations: the mother, her thirty-five-year-old son and twenty-year-old daughter, the son's wife, and their little boy, all in a place so small they have to share a bathroom with the neighbors, have to wake up early in the morning just so they can take a crap before somebody else gets in there. Because of job discrimination, the son, Walter Lee, has to work as a chauffeur, driving white folks around, which won't even pay for him to move somewhere with his wife and son. *He's* got a dream of opening up a liquor store. But what bank is going to lend money to Walter Lee? His dream gets deferred, and he's about ready to explode.

Walter Lee hopes his mama will lend him the money, though, because she's getting a check from an insurance company for her dead husband. At first his mama doesn't want to lend him the money. She says, "We ain't no business people. . . . We just plain working folks." And Walter Lee's wife tells her, "Ain't nobody business people till they go into business." And right there, that's one of the saddest things about people being beaten down: they think they're not *supposed* to do any better. *Ain't nobody business people till they go into business*—meaning just because you've never done something before, and you don't know other black people doing it, that doesn't mean *you* can't do it.

A Raisin in the Sun was the first play by a black woman to be performed on Broadway; that was in 1959. A few years later, Lorraine Hansberry died of cancer. Wasn't but thirty-four. She left behind a lesson for us, though.

Because, in the end, the play is about not giving up on yourself and not letting anybody tell you who you are or what you're worth. It's also about people taking care of one another.

Sidney Poitier Wins the Oscar for Best Actor for *Lilies of the Field*

Sidney Poitier grew up in the Bahamas. When he was born, in 1927, he didn't weigh but three pounds. One of seven children in a poor family. He said his mama made his clothes out of flour sacks. Sidney used to be embarrassed to go to school in clothes made from flour sacks, but his mama told him, "Don't worry about it. No shame in it. Long as the clothes are clean."

When he was a teenager, Sidney got in a little bit of trouble, so his father sent him to live with his older brother in Miami. Coming from the Bahamas, Sidney didn't know much about Jim Crow and white supremacists, but he got a quick education. Some white cops put a gun to his head—he hadn't done anything—and joked about whether they were going to shoot him in his right eye or his left. After that, he got out of Miami lickety-split and went to New York.

He landed in Harlem with three dollars in his pocket. He got a job as a dishwasher but didn't have a place to live, so just to feed himself, he joined the army. But because he respected himself and wasn't used to kissing up to white folks, he got into an altercation with a white officer and got kicked out. Back in New York, he got a job cleaning a theater, and that was how he started acting.

Sidney was smooth as silk on the screen—handsome, walking tall, just as dignified as you please. Folks said, "Hold on, what's *this?*" He was in the movie version of Lorraine Hansberry's play *A Raisin in the Sun*, in 1961. Before Sidney Poitier, only one African American had ever won an Oscar. In 1963, Sidney was in the movie *Lilies of the Field*, playing a dude who helps out some German-speaking nuns. And he won the Academy Award. What black folks who saw it never forgot, though, was his role in *In the Heat of the Night*, in 1967. He played a black cop who goes down south to investigate a murder. In one scene, he questions an old white dude. The dude doesn't like being questioned by a black man, so he slaps Sidney. In the movie script, Sidney's character was just supposed to look pissed off and walk out. But Sidney said, "Aw, *hell* no." Soon as that white dude slapped him, Sidney slapped him right back. And they kept it in the movie! Black people had never seen anything like it before. If there had been a black Oscar, he would've won it.

Motown, Diana Ross, and the Supremes

The Supremes was one of the biggest musical acts America had ever seen. In the 1960s they were just about as popular as the Beatles, and music groups don't *get* bigger than that. But you can't talk about the Supremes without talking about how the Motown record label got started.

The black man who started Motown, Berry Gordy Jr., was born in 1929 in Detroit. If you can take a lesson from Gordy's early life, it might be that you don't always succeed at the first thing you try, but that doesn't mean you won't succeed. He dropped out of high school to become a boxer, and he was pretty good, but not good enough to make it. Next, he went into the army. After that, he worked in his parents' print shop for a while, then tried to strike out on his own: he opened a record store that specialized in jazz. The customers didn't like jazz as much as he did, though, and the store folded. Then he became a factory worker, went to work for a Ford Motor plant. It was boring, dead-end work, but it ended up teaching him something.

He was still into music, though, and tried his hand at being a songwriter. Detroit had a great public music education program, and Gordy learned his way around songs and how they work. Meanwhile, he got married, then got divorced, then got married again. His second wife, Raynoma Liles, convinced him that he should *produce* records: not just write songs, but be in control of how they sounded when they were recorded. That basically meant being the boss of a record.

A number of things led Berry Gordy to start the Motown record label in 1959–60. One was that white singers liked to do covers of black people's music. Another was that after World War II, when folks had a little more money, white teenagers had some pocket change to spend. At first they bought the white singers' versions of black songs, but then a lot of them started to want the real thing. A third thing was that big bands were on their way out, and small groups were the thing. A fourth thing was that Berry Gordy knew the first three things. Finally, Gordy knew from his boring job at the Ford plant, and from his parents, how to make a business run right.

So, Gordy started his label in Detroit and got busy signing up acts. One of the first was the Miracles, with badass Smokey Robinson, who sang and wrote songs for the Miracles and a lot of other Motown people. Gordy's whole thing was to make records by black artists that were enough like pop songs to be crossover hits but enough like R&B songs to appeal to black folks. Gordy's plan worked, too. The singer Mary Wells had hits with songs like "My Guy," which Smokey wrote; and the Miracles came out with "Shop Around," which was a monster hit. Motown gave America a new sound.

Sports and singing were the gifts used by blacks for upward mobility. Detroit had a housing project, the Brewster-Douglass homes, and a lot of young people who lived there loved to sing. Two of them were Eddie Kendricks and Paul Williams, who were in a singing group called the Primes; they later became famous on the Motown label as the Temptations. Williams's girlfriend, Betty McGlown, loved to sing, too, and the Primes' manager had the idea of starting a girl group called the Primettes. Here's where you see the universe at work, adding the little touches that end up making the difference. Betty McGlown got her best friend, Mary Wilson, to be in the Primettes, along with Florence Ballard. Mary Wilson had a classmate who joined, too, almost as an afterthought. Her name was Diane Ross. Later she changed her first name to "Diana." She became the biggest one of them all—the brightest star in the Motown constellation and one of the most famous music stars there are.

The Primettes went to the Motown recording studios every day and bugged Berry Gordy until he let them be part of the label—in small ways at first, like clapping their hands and singing background for some of the other Motown singers. Then they became a Motown group themselves and changed their name to the Supremes. It took them a while to get a hit. But then they hooked up with a black songwriting team, Lamont Dozier and two brothers, Brian and Eddie Holland—together the three went by the name Holland-Dozier-Holland. That's how the Supremes became a hit machine, with songs like "Baby Love," "Stop! In the Name of Love," "Come See About Me," and "Back in My Arms Again."

Next thing you knew, the Supremes were everywhere: all over the radio, all over TV. Probably their most famous television appearances were on *The Ed Sullivan Show*, which was just about the biggest thing on television at the time. It started in December 1964. Betty McGlown had left the group by then, and Berry Gordy had decided that Diana Ross should be the lead singer. So, there were the Supremes, on black-and-white TV, with sleeveless knee-length dresses, Diana in the middle, Ballard and Wilson singing backup, all three of them dancing in place with enough hair on top of their heads for them and three other women besides. Folks went crazy hearing them.

When you listen to that group, they put a dignity in you so that every woman, black and white, knows that rhythm was fit for a queen. Thank you, Diana Ross and the Supremes.

And man, did they sound good!

Jimi Hendrix and "The Star-Spangled Banner"

Some black folks don't care about Jimi Hendrix because he played rock music instead of black music like soul or R&B. What they may not know, though, is that rock and roll came out of the blues, which is the blackest music there is. And Hendrix was just about the best guitar player there was.

If you were making up stories, you'd have a hard time coming up with a sadder one than the story of Jimi Hendrix's early life. He was born in Seattle, Washington, in 1942. His parents were alcoholics—his mother died of it when Jimi was fifteen—and the more they drank, the more they fought each other, till Jimi would run and hide. The little boy coped with his home life by playing guitar before he even *had* a guitar: he would pretend he was playing on a broom. After a while, his daddy gave him a ukulele that didn't have but one string. Jimi played that one string to death, though. He finally got a real guitar for five dollars, and then there was no stopping him. He practiced for hours a day. Talking about the blues, that's what Hendrix listened to when he was learning to play: blues musicians like Robert Johnson, B. B. King, Howlin' Wolf, and Muddy Waters. It goes to show you: we don't have to have much to create something powerful.

Hendrix got in a little trouble when he was young. The second time he was caught riding in a stolen car, they gave him a choice between prison and the army. He chose the army. He was so miserable in the service, though, that he begged his daddy to please send him his guitar. After he got out of the army, Jimi joined different bands and played on the Chitlin' Circuit, the clubs where blacks could put on shows, mostly in the South and along the East Coast. In early 1964, when he was twenty-one, he got a spot playing in the Isley Brothers' backup band. He was happy about that at first, but after a while, because he could play so well by then, he got tired of being somebody else's sideman.

He left the Isleys and moved to New York and then London, where he got a manager who organized a band to show off Hendrix's talent on the guitar. They called it the Jimi Hendrix

Experience. They were a hit over there. In 1967, they cut an album called *Are You Experienced*, which was one of the biggest records to come out of the 1960s. It was a mix of things: some of it was rock with weird sound effects and some of it was straight-up blues, and all of it showed off Hendrix's nimble-fingered guitar playing and his voice, which didn't sound like anybody else's. He played like a blues guitarist, if a blues guitarist had all that funny electronic feedback that the head-banging white rock musicians had. He had a sound all his own. In that same year, the group made the album *Axis: Bold as Love*, which was just as big, and in 1968 they made *Electric Ladyland*, which was even bigger.

In 1969, back in the United States, Hendrix headlined the four-day-long outdoor concert in Woodstock, New York. Almost half a million people went. Hendrix played the national anthem, "The Star-Spangled Banner"—his way. Francis Scott Key wrote "The Star-Spangled Banner" in 1814, but I don't think he could ever have imagined what Hendrix would one day do with it. Jimi didn't sing it; he just played it on electric guitar. He'd play one line of the song, and in between that and the next one, those fingers of his got to flying, making all that chugging, churning rock feedback. It was like he was saying, "They say America's one way, but listen to how it *really* is." People still talk about that performance. He didn't sing a word, but he said a whole lot.

Hendrix brings to mind the way Whitney Houston transformed the same song during Super Bowl XXV.

Ray Charles

Ray Charles gave millions of dollars to black colleges—not some chump change, but *millions*. One day, he and I were getting awards at Morehouse College, in Atlanta, Georgia. He was giving them four million dollars. I said, "Ray, I know you blind, you can't see, but you know how much money you just gave this school? You know it was four million, right?" He said, "Yeah, I know." I said, "I just want to make sure you knew, with your blind self."

Ray was into bringing about change in the times he was living in, and he was independent and strong enough to do that. He was also generous, but he was strong enough to say no at the right time. "No. I'm not doing this." Not everybody would do that, but Ray did. I'll give you an example. In 1961, he was supposed to play at the Bell Auditorium in Augusta, Georgia—till he found out that it was segregated. Whites could use the big dance floor, but blacks had to sit in the balcony. Ray didn't perform, and he told everybody *why* he wasn't performing, and then he left town. The promoter sued him, and Ray had to pay a fine, but he still wouldn't play in a segregated hall. That's who he was. He did play there the next year—after they'd desegregated it. That's the only time I like celebrities is when they consistently stand for something.

Man, what a human. He was born in 1930 in Georgia and grew up in Florida. Grew up poor. His mother wasn't but a teenager herself. Ray wasn't born blind; what was probably worse, he lost his sight gradually, and he lost it completely when he was around seven years old. His mama might have been young, but she had a little something on the ball. You might think that one good thing about going blind would be not having to do chores, but she made Ray do them anyway. The neighbors got on her about it, but she told them, "He's blind, not stupid." Being blind didn't mean he couldn't do things. Not only that, but she told him he had to do things for himself *and* other people.

When Ray was seven, his mother enrolled him at the Florida School for the Deaf and Blind. He started playing music there, and he learned to read music by reading Braille. He learned classical

music, but jazz, blues, and country were what really got him going. He started playing for money when he was a teenager, and in
1952, when he was twenty-one, he signed a contract with Atlantic
Records.

I think the reason Ray could sing and play blues, soul, gospel, *and*
country is because, at bottom, all those musical styles are about feeling, being able to express how you and other people feel. And Ray
could do that with his voice. You'd hear Ray sing and you'd know it
wasn't anybody else. It was like that from the beginning. Listen to
one of his early songs, "It Should Have Been Me." He sings about
seeing a guy with a "real fine chick" and thinking, "It shoulda been
me, with that real fine chick"—and what dude hasn't thought *that*?
Meanwhile, the song makes you want to snap your fingers. He could
also sing about having a woman and being in love, like in "I Got
a Woman" and "Hallelujah, I Love Her So," which were a couple
of his hits from the 1950s. For singing about being in love, though,
nothing topped his song from 1962, "I Can't Stop Loving You." He
almost sounded like he was singing about a woman when he made
"Georgia on My Mind," in 1960. Same with his version of "America
the Beautiful." The way he sang it, he almost made you believe it!

When I got to know him, I found out he had been doing good
stuff for the cause. If there was a civil rights fund-raiser somewhere, somebody would say, "Hey, man, let's see if we can get Ray
Charles to play," and maybe he would, but usually if you called Ray
Charles about something like that, he'd send you a *check*.

Richard Pryor and Comic Geniuses

I tell it like I see it, and I see it like this: if you're talking about the
three greatest comic super geniuses on the planet, two of them were
white: Mark Twain and Lenny Bruce.

But I see it this way, too. You name any field, and there's going to be a black person in it somewhere. And not just in it, but doing it *right*, showing other folks how it's done. That's one of the miraculous things about us, considering all we've been through. And it's true about comedy, too, because the third name is Richard Pryor.

Richard Pryor's grandmother ran a whorehouse, and his mother was a whore. Now, you might not think somebody would feel dignity or pride over that. But in the black community, that made you a big shot, because people see all these important white men showing up where you live, since the whorehouse was there for the benefit of white men. For most folks, especially poor folks, the biggest thing in your life might be that Mr. So-and-So who owns Such-and-Such came by the ghetto. So, that kind of made Richard Pryor important when he was growing up. But when he hit it big, and all that became public knowledge nationwide, it wasn't a source of pride for him anymore.

Through all of it, the stories that came out about his family, the fame, and all the rest, you never saw anybody more bashful in your life than Richard Pryor—when he wasn't onstage and the camera was off. When it came on, watch out. Get out the way. How do you explain that? It was there all the time, pinned in.

You listen to Richard Pryor, and just his voice itself makes you laugh, because he sounds like he can't believe what he's telling you himself. There was a lot of pain in some of what he said. Humbleness, too. And he could get all that across in a way that would make you laugh until tears were streaming down your face. That's genius. Sometimes he'd say something, and it would be funny, but you'd have to think a minute before you realized how deep it was. A good example: In 1982 he did a record and movie called *Live on the Sunset Strip*. (The record won a Grammy Award.) One of the stories he told on that record was about going to Africa and seeing black people everywhere, and how everybody he saw looked like a black person he knew back home. He said, "The winos I knew here . . . over there, they're diplomats! Look at this mother! That's what he's *supposed* to be!" He made you laugh saying it, because his voice was so funny, and then he'd start talking about something else, but you'd think about it a minute, and you'd realize he was *right*.

I was talking about Mark Twain, the writer. *That* was a funny dude, but like Richard Pryor, he had some serious stuff to say, and a lot of it had to do with black folks. He wrote *The Adventures of Huckleberry Finn*. In that book, a black man had a first name, Jim. Otherwise, back then, most black characters were "So-and-So's nigger," but *this black man's name was Jim*. And when you read that book, you'll see that when Nigger Jim and the white boy, Huck, go fishing, Jim isn't out there fishing for Huck. He isn't going to catch the fish and bone it and fry it for that white boy. He is out there for him*self*. That was the first time in America you had a *normal conversation* between a black man and a white man.

Then, after that, Twain kept it rolling when he wrote *Pudd'nhead Wilson*. Wow, man. Check this out: one of the characters is a woman named Roxy, who looks white but is a slave, because she's *one-sixteenth black*, and she talks like a slave, because that's how she's been brought up. She has a baby, a boy, by a white man. At the same time, Roxy's master has a baby son. Now, the two boys live in the same house and look almost alike—the only one who can tell them apart is Roxy—but because her son is *one-thirty-second black*, she knows he's in danger of being sold down the river one day. So, she figures that the best way to protect her son is to switch the babies. From then on, her son is raised as the master's white son, and the master's white son is a slave called a nigger. The white boy acts and talks and thinks like a nigger, and the boy who's thirty-one parts white and one part black grows up as arrogant and mean and racist as anybody you ever saw. Then, when Roxy's real son is grown and she tells him he's black, for a while he starts to *act* that way, flinching away from white folks like he's doing something wrong just by being in their presence.

Think about that a minute. What's Twain saying? When you start to untangle it, you realize he's saying some heavy stuff. For one thing, for as much as white folks carried on at the time about the separation of the races, after the sun went down, it was a different story. Almost nobody knew it, but the father of Roxy's baby was a *prominent* white man, and he wasn't the only one sneaking around with black folks. A lot of real-life white folks did that, too, beginning with slave masters, which is why black folks come in so many shades. Then you think about how Roxy's son and the other boy acted and were treated based on what race they and other people *thought* they were. And you understand some of the absurdity of what we're dealing with.

Then there was Lenny Bruce. He was like Mark Twain: he would call things what they were. And talk about funny. You could drop a glass in the nightclub where he was performing, and he'd do forty brilliant minutes just about *that*. Now, Lenny was Jewish, but that didn't stop him from saying whatever he wanted to say. In the early 1960s, when they were having the trial for the Nazi Adolf Eichmann, Lenny sat on the stage and did his little bit, and then, suddenly, the stage was lit up in red. Then he raised his head up and said, "My name is Adolph Eichmann. You Americans tried me and sentenced me to death. Like I did something that you didn't do. You're the same as me. Yes I killed Americans, I killed Jews. What a thrill I had killin' ya, skinnin' ya. Putting cigarettes in your eyes. I made lampshades out of your skin. My defense . . . I was a soldier. Do you people think you're better because you burn your enemies at long distance with missiles, without ever seeing what you've done to them. You dropped the nuclear bomb on Hiroshima. You didn't get to smell the flesh burning. You didn't hear them scream. You cowards." Lenny went on: "I was in the room. I got to snatch their teeth out. The dogs that were biting them—we put false teeth on 'em that would cut through the nervous system, but y'all just thought they were ordinary dogs!"

One day, Scotland Yard, the British police, came to visit Lenny. They said, "We like to look at ourselves as a liberal nation. There's a big demand for you to come and play London. The Palladium. So, we okayed it. But we want to let you know: if you say *anything* about the queen, we're going to beat you right there onstage and then throw you in jail." Lenny said, "Oh, I would never do that." When he went over there to perform, the place was packed. Lenny walked onstage, and the first thing that crazy dude said was, "Did y'all know that Queen Elizabeth gave Winston Churchill the clap?" And Scotland Yard did what they said they were going to do.

(Now, that doesn't have anything to do with black folks, but it's funny, right?)

Stevie Wonder and *Songs in the Key of Life*

Stevie Wonder—he's on a whole other level. He shouldn't even be talked about in the same breath as most entertainers. Stevie can do two things at once. He'll write and play songs that'll get your hips moving. But then it's also like his music is on a higher plane. It's like, because he's blind, he's looking *in* instead of *out*, and what's in his mind is a musical landscape nobody else has ever seen. And he shares it with us, one song at a time.

He was born in 1950. Unlike Ray Charles, who went blind in childhood, Stevie never had any sight—he was born premature and had a condition that caused his retinas to detach. Now, folks argue about "nature versus nurture." Some say people are the way they are because of how they're raised. Others say you're just born the way you are. Stevie's a good argument for the nature side. Here's a blind kid who starts playing piano, drums, and harmonica, and playing them *right*, too. All the raising in the world won't produce *that* if it's not already in you.

Stevie wasn't but eleven years old when he signed a contract with Motown. The thing people forget about Stevie is that, because he was so young when he started, he still wasn't but in his early twenties when his music really started to get mature. He did some good music in the 1960s. He had a hit singing and playing drums and harmonica on "Fingertips," which was released right after he turned thirteen, and he did songs like "Uptight (Everything's Alright)" in the mid-1960s. But then came the early 1970s. When he was twenty-one, twenty-two, and twenty-three, a time of life when most people don't have one single idea about what they're doing, Stevie released albums: *Music of My Mind* in 1972, *Talking Book* later that same year, and *Innervisions* the year after that. *Talking Book* had "Superstition" on it. Here's a twenty-two-year-old telling you:

> *When you believe in things that you don't understand,*
> *Then you suffer,*
> *Superstition ain't the way*

—and making you dance at the same time! *Innervisions* had "Higher Ground." Check it out:

> *I'm so darn glad he let me try it again*
> *'Cause my last time on Earth I lived a whole world of sin.*

I'm so glad that I know more than I knew then,
Gonna keep on tryin'
Till I reach the highest ground

This is from a twenty-two-year-old! *Innervisions* had "Living for the City," too, which is like a novel in a song. And then came *Fulfillingness' First Finale* in 1974, with "Boogie on Reggae Woman" and "You Haven't Done Nothin'" on it. If you can sit still while "You Haven't Done Nothin'" is playing, somebody needs to come bury you.

He could have stopped there, and his reputation would have been made. But then, in 1976, he came out with *Songs in the Key of Life*. That album was like Stevie saying, "You think you've seen my talent? Check *this* out, y'all." One of the songs on it, "Sir Duke," starts out, "Music is a world within itself." Well, *Songs in the Key of Life* is a world within itself. It has so many moods. There's joyfulness and celebration in "Sir Duke" and a deeper joy in "Isn't She Lovely"; there's nostalgia for childhood in "I Wish"; there's sorrow in "Village Ghetto Land"; there's a history lesson with a groove in "Black Man"; and Stevie's giving you something to think about in "Pastime Paradise."

Stevie's *aware*, too. He gives his time to the cause, and he had a whole campaign in 1980 to make Martin Luther King Jr.'s birthday a national holiday.

And what you've got to love about Stevie is his kindness, his pleasantness. The only thing about him I'd say is: if he could just see one time, and see what kind of outfits these folks have him wearing onstage, he'd fire them *all*!

One of the things I love most about Stevie Wonder is that he has always stood for what was right, even when it affected his pocket. In 2013, Stevie publically announced that he was boycotting Florida following the murder of young Trayvon Martin and the acquittal of his murderer George Zimmerman. Stevie said that he refused to perform in the state of Florida until its stand-your-ground law was abolished. Even said that he wouldn't perform in any other states that recognized that law. He lost all that money and never talks about it. That's who he is.

Death of Marvin Gaye

Marvin Gaye—man, what a beautiful brotha. You never met a kinder, more gentle, and more loving human being than he was. But what happened to him was so sad. Leading up to his death, his behavior was so unpredictable that I believe the mob was trying to control him by supplying him with drugs. I'd go out to Marvin's house sometimes, and Marvin and a bunch of guys would be playing ball all day, and I just never associated being hooked on drugs with having all that physical energy. But that was Marvin.

A couple of times I carried him to my farm and cleaned him out. One time, Marvin was going to do a concert in Philly or Washington, DC. I said I'd take him home with me that night, after the concert. He said he just didn't feel like going. So, I told him, "Then I'm going home with you."

Now, what happened that angered me so bad was this: When I went home with Marvin, I saw all this white powdery stuff on a table at his place. I found him in another room and told him what I'd seen. I said, "Man, what are you doing?" He started complaining about how the maids had left some cleanser on the table, like I'd never seen cocaine before. Then he said, "I hope you didn't throw it away." (Yeah, it'd be a shame if I threw that spilled cleanser away.) Anyway, I just said, "What I'll do is tomorrow I'll go to the health food store and buy you the combination of stuff that I use to help with detoxification." The next day, when I made to go out to get him some of my sobriety concoction, he said, "Here, go over and ask the money man, the white boy, to give you the money." I found the dude he was talking about. White boy. He said, "Dick Gregory. Oh Dick—love you, man. Wow. Wow. Can I help you?"

I said, "Marvin told me to come over and get some money. I'm going to the health food store. I didn't want to come over, but—"

Soon as I said the word *money*, that was the end of the "Oh, Dick, I love you" BS. The white guy said, "Marvin doesn't have the right to ask for money."

So, I went back to Marvin and said, "Why'd you humiliate me like that? I got a pocketful of money, man. I don't have to ask some white boy for money 'cause you sent me, and then have him tell me you don't have a right to ask for nothing." I called Lil, my wife, and said, "If Marvin calls me, don't even tell me he called."

Then—*pow*. Lil called a few days later and said, "Marvin's just been killed." That was April 1, 1984. Then his main people called me, and the dude told me, "Lil was trying to get you 'cause Marvin said, 'If Gregory doesn't come to get me outta the house, my daddy'll probably kill me.'"

Now let me tell you the story.

What happened was, Marvin's daddy was a *pedophile*. And he had two little boys he was bringing to the house, where Marvin's mother was dying from cancer. Marvin was there in his pajamas giving his mother some medicine when his daddy came in.

So, Marvin said to his daddy, "You can't do this," meaning bring boys there.

Marvin's daddy went off. He told Marvin, "F**k you, this is my house! You gave this house to her"—meaning Marvin's mother. I guess he thought that made the house *his*. "I don't believe you my son anyway. That woman is going to bed with every nigger out there. You ain't my son. That's why you give everything to her and you ain't never give nothin' to me." And Marvin hit his daddy, and his daddy went and got the gun—and *pow*.

Maybe the only surprising part about Marvin being killed by his daddy was that it took so long to happen.

Marvin was born in Washington, DC, in 1939, the second of four kids, and almost from the beginning, his daddy (who was a minister!) started beating on him. Marvin sang from an early age, and that, together with his mama's encouragement, kept him sane. He still had his daddy to deal with, though. When Marvin was in his teens, things with his daddy got so bad that Marvin Sr. used to kick him out of the house. Marvin joined the air force, but didn't like that too much, so when he came home again, he went back to singing.

He made his way to Detroit, where he met Berry Gordy of Motown; he became a session musician, playing drums, before releasing records of his own. At first it looked like he couldn't *give* them away, but then, in 1962, he came out with the song "Stubborn Kind of Fellow," and there was no stopping him after that. He sang duets with Kim Weston, on "It Takes Two," and Tammi Terrell, on "Ain't No Mountain High Enough" and "Ain't Nothing Like the Real Thing."

Then came Marvin's megahits. He recorded "I Heard It Through the Grapevine" in 1968 and "What's Going On" in 1971, and if anybody hadn't heard of him before that, they sure knew who he was afterward. Then, in 1973, he put out the album *Let's Get It On*, which was about exactly what it sounds like. Maybe only Marvin could have gotten away with that title. Then he did it again, in 1982, with the song "Sexual Healing," on his album *Midnight Love*. That was his biggest hit of all.

Two years later came the tragedy with his daddy, and it was all over.

After he died, Marvin's sister called me and said, "We're holding things up till you give us the okay. Would you come out here and do the funeral?" It was bittersweet to be given the honor of eulogizing one of my dearest friends.

You can still hear Marvin's records—hear that ache of desire in his voice when he sings "Let's Get It On," hear that pleading in his soul when he calls for peace and love in "What's Going On." He influenced a lot of singers, touched a lot of people. I hope my brotha has found some peace.

The Cosby Show

I mean the Cosby "show" in more ways than one.

When the show *I Spy* hit TV in 1965, it was the first time in the history of this planet that a black man could stop, pull out a gun, and shoot. And he could shoot a white man. I had never seen that. Neither had anybody else. Everybody had seen white boys do it—all you had to do was turn on a TV, day or night, and see that—but a *black* man? People saw that and said, "Man! What is this?" Before that, black folks had to wrap their guns in twelve towels and put them under the car seat. That's why they couldn't shoot nobody but other black people; because by the time you finished unwrapping all that stuff, those white boys you were mad at were gone. But that was the whole thing about *I Spy*: it was comical, because Cosby was a funny guy, but it was powerful, too. And it couldn't have worked the same way with two black men, because when you saw Cosby and Robert Culp together, you saw they were *equals*. They were government agents, traveling all over the world. They posed as a tennis player and his trainer, but they were packing heat, and they could *use* it.

Only thing about it was: wherever they went, Culp always got the girl. That's why Cosby told his stand-up audience one time, "I want to film *I Spy* in Africa. Bob Culp wouldn't get the girl then!" That cracked me up.

The Cosby Show debuted on NBC in 1984. It went straight to number one. It became bigger than life. But it still didn't threaten white people. See, white folks were already in love with Bill Cosby. Little white children were riding on his back eating Jell-O, eating tapioca out of his ears. He didn't become a threat until later.

Now you've got the whole mess with Cosby being accused of raping women. I condone none of this. Women are God's gift to the world. I do pray for him and his family that the truth will come out. Now, I'm not going to tell you he did or he didn't. But think about this: why are they talking about jail time for Cosby when no other rich person goes to jail for doing anything? Athletes can do anything they want to do, and nothing happens to them. Big business pays the government billions of dollars in penalties for this or that crime, but they don't even have to admit they broke a law. And *nobody goes to jail.*

In the 1990s, Bill Cosby was getting ready to buy NBC. White supremacy came in and said no. You see, there's a thing called racist white folks giving what I call a liberation holiday. That's when white folks throw us a bone. That's what Cosby's show was. When you put this show on, and it shows black folks doing well, white folks can't wait to watch it. Then the racists can say, "What are you blacks complaining about? Cosby went to school and got a good education. What's wrong with the rest of you?" The kids on that show had to be better than white kids just to be accepted. They'd go to fancy places like art galleries on Saturday, all dressed up—while rich white folks were wearing cutoff jeans and going to the park. That's what you call a liberation holiday. That was the game. But that's all white supremacy wanted us to have: a show.

When Bill Cosby was negotiating to buy NBC, and get some

real power and put on the kinds of shows *he* wanted to put on, *that's* when white supremacy killed his son. They said he was robbed and killed on the highway. Think again. Ask yourself a question: if white children on the Jell-O pudding commercials loved Cosby so much, how come he couldn't get a commercial after his son was killed? No more Jell-O commercials—but Cosby didn't kill anybody, and neither did his son. What's this about? Cosby knew something that most folks didn't know. That Mercedes he bought his son had reboots—you get a flat, it reboots itself. But they said Cosby's son was stopped on the highway because he had a flat. Why? Cosby knew that wasn't what really happened. Do you really think Cosby's son got out of his car to call a white woman, and she showed up in a mink coat, miniskirt, and high-heel shoes to help him change a flat, when all he had to do was push a button and the flat would have changed itself? Bill Cosby knew that. If you look at the police report—and I read the whole thing—there was no robbery. That's why they called it an *attempted* robbery and a *failed* robbery. When his body was found, Cosby's son had six thousand dollars in cash, all his credit cards, and his cell phone on him. No robbery. Then, six months later, they arrested an American who was a Russian immigrant and charged him with the killing. But when we checked, it turned out that guy was in Mexico the night of the killing. Bill Cosby knows all this.

Michael Jordan's father was killed on the side of the road, too. Sound familiar?

Toni Morrison Wins the Nobel Prize for Literature

In 1993, Toni Morrison won the biggest prize a writer can win: the Nobel Prize in Literature.

Toni Morrison was born Chloe Ardelia Wofford in 1931 in Ohio. Her parents were part of the Great Migration; they had come to Ohio to escape the South. But they brought a little of the South with them, and when Morrison was growing up, they told her stories from down there—black folk tales. So, storytelling was part of her life from the beginning.

People know Toni Morrison as a writer, but she started out doing other things. After getting her bachelor's degree in English from Howard University and her master's from Cornell, she taught at Texas Southern University and then Howard. After that, she became a book editor at the biggest place there is for a book editor to work: Random House. She signed up a whole lot of black writers, like Toni Cade Bambara and Angela Davis.

Then, in the early 1970s, she started writing books herself. When she was in college and graduate school, she studied the works of William Faulkner, and just as the sentences in Faulkner's novels are almost musical, Toni Morrison's writing has a musical quality to it, too. You read her sentences and you see and feel a rhythm going on. Her novels are *The Bluest Eye, Sula, Song of Solomon, Tar Baby, Beloved, Jazz, Paradise, Love, A Mercy, Home,* and *God Help the Child.* A lot of her novels are set in the past, early in the twentieth century or even in the nineteenth. They're about black families, relationships between men and women, and the past coming back to haunt you. Mostly, though, they're about how black people *live,* how we talk, how we feel, how we hurt, how we love, how we respond to racism, how we *are.* Some of the books have supernatural things going on, just like in some of the black folk tales her family told her when she was growing up. Guess the girl was listening.

Talking about how black folks feel: In *Beloved,* not far from the end, two characters are talking. One is called Paul D. The other is called Stamp Paid. (That sista can sure come up with some names for her characters.) So, Paul D has seen and been through a lot. He says to Stamp Paid, "Tell me this one thing. How much is a nigger supposed to take? Tell me. How much?" Stamp Paid says, "All he can." And Paul D comes back at him with the best response—really, the *only* response: "Why? Why? Why? Why? Why?"

And right there, Toni Morrison nails it, because at the bottom, that's what it all comes down to—all the pain and frustration, all the mess black folks have to deal with. You have to struggle three times as hard as anybody else just to make it through the day.

Mae Jemison

I keep saying it, and I'll keep on saying it: anywhere you go, there's a black person kicking ass. The thing about it is you can't wait until there's already a black person kicking ass somewhere before you decide to go there and kick some yourself. Doesn't have to be like basketball, where you know a hundred other black guys are trying to do it, so you figure it's okay for you to do it, too. Sometimes you've got to be the first. Shirley Chisholm didn't see any black women running for president before she decided to do it. The way she told it was "Somebody had to do it first." So, the next time you think about doing something, and you hear somebody say, "Aw, man, black people don't do stuff like that," think about Shirley Chisholm. And think about Mae Jemison.

When Mae Jemison was growing up in Chicago in the 1950s and '60s, she didn't see any black astronauts or female astronauts. For one good reason: they didn't exist. That didn't stop her from wanting to be one. And she didn't just want to be an astronaut; she *knew* she was going to be one. That's the kind of confidence black folks need in this world. But she also knew it wasn't going to happen by itself, and that's why she worked her tail off.

She got into Stanford University on a National Achievement Scholarship and was in her last year there when the National Aeronautics and Space Administration, NASA, put out a call for civilians to apply to the space program, especially women and minorities. Now, Mae Jemison could have applied right there, but she knew two things. One was, as determined as she felt, the competition was stiff, so she'd better have a backup plan. Another was that the more impressive she made herself, the better the chances that they'd pick her.

So that sista made herself into one impressive human being. She went to Cornell University Medical College and became a doctor. Then she joined the Peace Corps, working as a medical officer in Sierra Leone and Liberia. Wasn't but twenty-six years old. She looked like a kid, and folks over there tried to treat her like one, but she let them know what kind of person they were dealing with.

Then she came back to the United States and applied to NASA—she and two thousand other folks. And she made it. That's how she became the first black woman to get accepted to NASA's astronaut program. A few years after that, in 1992, she went into space on the shuttle *Endeavor.* Stayed up there eight days, doing all kinds of experiments related to weightlessness and motion sickness in space.

Several other black astronauts are Leland Melvin, Robert Satcher, and Stephanie Wilson, among others. So, when you're counting the places where black folks are kicking ass, you can add outer space to the list. And that's good, because you're not getting *my* black behind up there.

Maya Angelou

Most people know that Jesse Owens ran like nobody's business and Jackie Robinson was the first black baseball player in the Major Leagues. They kept it simple. Some folks, though, do so many things in their careers that a lot of people don't know what they were best known for, because there's not just one simple thing to focus on. Here's an example for you: Melvin Van Peebles. That brotha has been a movie director *and* a novelist *and* a playwright *and* a composer *and*—you ready for this one?—a Wall Street trader.

Maya Angelou might be another example, except everybody knows she wrote *I Know Why the Caged Bird Sings*, a book about her life. And most people know she recited her poem "On the Pulse of Morning" at Bill Clinton's presidential inauguration in 1993. But like Melvin, you almost don't know what to focus on with Maya because her gifts were so vast. People should know what she did, though, because she was something else.

What happened to her when she was a child has been told before, but it's worth telling again. She was born in 1928 in Missouri. Her name was Marguerite Johnson, but she got the name "Maya" because her older brother called her "My-a sister." When she was three her parents split up, and her daddy sent her and her brother to live with their grandmother in Arkansas. This was during the Depression, but her grandma was one of the few black people around who had any money, because she owned a general store. She lent money to black folks *and* white folks. A few years later, Maya's daddy came through again, and this time he took the kids to live with their mother in St. Louis. When Maya was eight, she was molested by her mom's boyfriend. She didn't tell anybody except her brother, but he told the rest of the family, and a while later the boyfriend was killed, probably by Maya's uncles. Maya stopped talking after that, because she thought it was her words that had gotten the man killed. That's some heavy stuff to put on a child.

Over the years, she and her brother kept moving around— first they went back to their grandmother's, then to their mother's place, in California this time. When they were living with their grandmother, Maya met a teacher who got her interested in books, and that helped her to speak again.

Then, in California, before she'd even finished high school, she started living all those lives I mentioned. She became the first female streetcar conductor in San Francisco. Then, when she was seventeen, she became a mother. She worked a lot of jobs to support herself and her son, including being a prostitute. (She was open about that stuff later on, too.) She was married for three years in the early 1950s and moved to New York City to study dance. She even performed in a nightclub, dancing to calypso music; that's when she started calling herself Maya Angelou. *Then* she was in *Porgy and Bess* in Europe, and *then* she made a calypso album.

I'm getting tired just telling you about it all, and she wasn't even half-finished yet.

In the late 1950s, Maya started writing, and she also got involved in the civil rights movement after hearing Martin Luther King Jr. speak. She worked with King's Southern Christian Leadership Conference—but in the North. In the 1960s she acted in the play *The Blacks, and* she lived in Africa and worked as a journalist, *and* she got tight with Malcolm X, *and* she made a TV documentary about black Americans and Africa, called *Blacks, Blues, Black!*

I'm running out of breath, but that sista wasn't done yet.

I'm getting to the stuff everybody knows about, though. At one point, she became friends with the writer James Baldwin, who encouraged her writing, and she published her book *I Know Why the Caged Bird Sings.* As many things as she had done, *that's* what really made her famous. She was just getting started as a writer, though. By the time she died, in 2014, she'd written six more books of autobiography: *Gather Together in My Name, Singin' and Swingin' and Gettin' Merry Like Christmas, The Heart of a Woman, All God's Children Need*

Traveling Shoes, A Song Flung Up to Heaven, and *Mom & Me & Mom.* She published a whole bunch of poetry, too, classic, extraordinary poetry. With all her accomplishments, they ran out of awards and honorary degrees to give her. They almost had to start some new colleges so there'd be more degrees for her.

The Death of Michael Jackson

Michael died at two o'clock in the morning. He was killed by a laser, and nobody has lasers but the government. Now, the doctor, the black guy they accuse of killing him, Conrad Murray—you know he did only two years of jail time? You kill the most famous human being on the planet and that's all you get? What does that tell you? He wasn't the one who did it.

Now, let's look at Michael. Michael watched James Brown. For twenty-nine years he studied him. No envy, no bitterness, just watching, and then one day he slipped from that twenty-nine years of studying to do the moonwalk—and brought things to a whole other level.

Now, I haven't got a single grandchild, one and a half years old or twenty, who can't out-moonwalk Michael Jackson, because once you put it out there, whether it's the moonwalk or the fastest hundred-yard dash in history, somebody else will come along and top you. But Michael was the *first*.

Michael was the only top, top, *top* entertainer who had a black accountant. In 1985, Michael bought Associated Television, which owned the Beatles songbook, for $47.5 million. When they killed him, it was worth close to $1 billion.

But to back up a minute: shortly before he died, Michael was rehearsing. He was supposed to do fifty shows in the City of London. That's BS—nobody could do that. He was insured for $17.5 million with Lloyd's of London. Now, think about this for a minute. If he had died, there wouldn't have been a show. It's not like there was an understudy they could have brought in. (Can you imagine that? There would have been riots that made LA in '92 look like a Catholic Mass.) Michael *was* the show. So, Lloyd's of London put all that money on something that depended on one person—and you're telling me they didn't look at him long enough to see the needle holes in his arms? (I'll explain those needle marks in a minute.)

Now, before *that*, we go back to the accusations against Michael—all those lies they told about him. That little white dentist Evan Chandler, he sued Michael because, he said, Michael had allegedly fondled his son. What really happened was this: Chandler was a screenwriter. He said to Michael, "I've got a couple of movies I'd like you to help me make." Michael said, "I'm not interested," and *that's* when the dentist said to his son, "Michael fondled you." Next thing you know, there's a trial in California.

Around that time, Michael's mother and daddy called me up. "This is Joe," his dad said. "Me and my wife want you to come out here. Michael's dying." They knew Michael would let me upstairs to see him, even though he was refusing all visitors. That's how close Michael and I were.

The day the trial was over, before the verdict came in, I was in the car with Michael. We got to his house, and he was so upset he went right upstairs. When I went into his room he hugged me and whispered, "I'm scared."

I said, "When was the last time you had some water?"

"I haven't. They'll poison me."

I said, "When was the last time you ate?"

"I can't eat."

He needed somebody to help him, so that's what I tried to do. I knew somebody who had a special kind of machine; she came down that night and used it to test Michael, and she said he was dying of dehydration. I said to Michael, "You're dehydrated. Here's what we'll do. I'm going to take you somewhere else. We can't let a hospital know you're coming, but we'll take you to San Francisco, and just walk in a hospital that doesn't know we're coming."

So, we got in the car and drove to the hospital. (When we pulled up to the door, we saw the car that had been following us pull over.) The hospital staff hooked Michael up at 5:30 that day. At 6:00 the next morning they were still giving him intravenous fluids. The doctor said: twelve more hours, and Michael would've been dead.

Once he was stabilized, Michael now had time to go to my farm. After that, the press all over the world said how good he looked. "Oh, doesn't he looked good."

Michael had a sadness about him. He was like a sad child, with all those animals. One time, I'm sitting up there and I see Michael's got this chimp in a baby bed. I thought it was a stuffed chimp. Another time, I slept out there one night and I looked up, and there was a giraffe looking through my window. That place was like a fairy tale.

Michael would try to pay me back for things. I'd tell him, "What do I need your money for? Go buy you some lollypops or something." Once, he gave me the code to the hotel where he was staying in New York. I went in, and he dimmed all the lights, put mics around, and talked to me for two days. He'd say, "Tell me about blackness. Tell me about love." Like a child.

Then came the day Michael died, June 25, 2009. Found dead in his bed. Around noon that day, his doctor called 911. *He didn't even know Michael's address.* You hear me? Now, you can Google that. Michael's own doctor had to go get somebody else to give the medical team the address.

When the first responders got there (within ten minutes), they didn't know Michael was already dead. They thought that whatever had happened to him had *just* happened. So, they started in with all kinds of lifesaving measures, including pumping his chest. Now, the people who had gotten to Michael—this is how clever they were: the first responders had to go back outside and get the drugs that they shot into his arms to try to revive him. They were helping the cover-up without even knowing that's what they were doing. They were injecting him and injecting him because they were trying to save him. *That's* where the needle marks came from.

Now, let's go back to Lloyd's of London. For a $17.5 million insurance policy, what kind of exam did they give him that they didn't find those drugs in his body? See how simple it is? *Seventeen point five million dollars!* Man, if a wino tries to get a job at the post office, they can track the stuff he's been taking. But that's how the marks got there. Nobody denied they were there. And then Deepak Chopra came out and said, "Every time Michael Jackson came to my clinic, he wanted me to give him that drug." That's when I suspected Chopra was working for the government. He's claiming he had a personal relationship with Michael, and then he holds a press conference and says Michael was asking him to give him that stuff?

Michael's will says he left his money to his mom (not his dad), his three children, and somebody else. Check this out: *Not one of his three children's names was their full birth name.* So how could Michael have signed that? Plus, the day he was supposed to have signed the policy in LA, he was in New York City with Al Sharpton.

The will read that if anybody Michael had left money to tried to bring a lawsuit over the policy and lost, they would not see any money. So that was when Michael's mom (whom he loved dearly) realized there was something wrong. She went to court. The people behind all this knew they had a winner. The whole thing was a fraud, but when you've got a government coming after you, you have no way to win. The government is the same one that drops bombs and wins wars.

It's hard to calculate what the world lost when it lost Michael. He had a magic about him from the time he was a little boy. There's no way in the world a ten-year-old boy ought to be able to sing that well, but he did, and even when he was onstage with his four good-looking older brothers, the only person you wanted to watch was Michael. I think for black kids coming up when the Jackson 5 hit it big, it was as if *they* were Michael. In Jackson 5 songs from the late 1960s and early '70s—"ABC," "I Want You Back," "I'll Be There," and "The Love You Save"—Michael was singing everything about love that those kids were feeling; it was as if his voice was their voice. Not just black kids, either—black folks alone couldn't have made Michael Jackson the biggest entertainer of all time. Black people, white people, people all over the *world* adored that brother, plastic surgery, bleached skin, and all—they loved him for the excitement he made them feel. Man, it's hard to find words to describe how big he was as a solo artist starting in the 1970s and especially the 1980s, with the albums *Off the Wall*, *Bad*, and the granddaddy of them all, *Thriller*.

And *dancing?* You never saw anybody dance like that. When he did the moonwalk, sliding backward like that, it was like he carried around his own special gravity.

Michael was born in 1958 and grew up in Gary, Indiana. He wasn't but five or six when he started performing with his brothers. Their daddy used to sit there with a belt while they were rehearsing, and the brothers knew what would happen if they didn't do it right. You could say that messed Michael up as a person, and you probably wouldn't be wrong.

John H. Johnson and *Ebony* and *Jet* Magazines

Let me tell you a story about *Jet* magazine.

In the late 1970s, I went to the African country Uganda, which was falling apart under Idi Amin. His rule was over, and he had left a mess. I wanted to see about helping sick and hungry folks over there. I got on a plane and then onto a bus. Things were crazy over there, with people fighting for control of the country. A group of men made everybody get off the bus I was on. And the saddest thing was: suddenly I was looking at a nine-year-old African child with a gun, who walked up to me and said, "Get up on the sidewalk."

A man on a bicycle jumped off and said, "Dick Gregory! Dick Gregory!" He looked at that little punk packing the gun and said, "Get outta here. You know who this man is?"

And how did the *man on the bicycle* know who I was? *Jet* magazine.

That man said to me, "I see all your work, brotha. I just . . ." And he started crying. Because he had read about me in *Jet*.

Jet and *Ebony* magazines exposed black people to the world—not just the negativity, but the positive things, too. We got to see black folks we had never seen, hear about black folks we had never heard of. Let's say your sister was a judge. How would I know that? Because *Jet* magazine put it out there. Let's say your daddy was a scientist in California, but I'm in New York. How would I know? The *New York Times* wouldn't mention it. So we looked at *Jet* and said, "Wow, this is positive stuff, not just the negative stuff about black folks that the white press was talking about." *Ebony* and *Jet* had black photographers taking pictures of people and things that white photographers wouldn't even have thought of.

Now the little black girl in Topeka can aspire to be a judge—not just because your sister's a judge, but because the little girl read about her in *Jet*. She doesn't know your sister, but she doesn't have to. Black folks would frame the covers of *Jet* and *Ebony* magazine.

And who started all that? John H. Johnson. He started out poor, grandson of slaves, and before he died, in 2005, he was the first African American to make *Forbes* magazine's list of the four hundred wealthiest Americans. Because he had a *vision*.

He was born in 1918 in Arkansas. Where he grew up, the schools were segregated, and the town didn't even have a high school for blacks. How do you like that? They'd rather he didn't go to school at all than go to school with white folks. Instead of just dropping out, though, Johnson repeated the eighth grade. That's how much he wanted an education.

When he was a teenager, he and his mother went to Chicago, to the World's Fair—his father had died in a mill accident—and they liked it so much that they decided to stay. Then Johnson's stepfather moved there, too. Johnson could attend high school there, and not only was he a good student, but he was editor of the student newspaper.

The year Johnson graduated from high school, 1936, the Urban League had a dinner, and Johnson was one of the speakers. One of the people listening was Harry Pace, president of the Supreme Liberty Life Insurance Company. Johnson impressed Pace so much that Pace gave him a job: editor of the company's magazine.

Black folks were the ones who had insurance policies with the company. When Johnson was putting the magazine together, he made sure to include stories he had found in other publications, stories about blacks. Then, after a while, he got an idea. What if he started his own magazine for black people? Like every other business idea, this one called for some money. He asked his mother for

help, and she made him get a $500 loan, with her furniture as se-
curity. So now Johnson *had* to succeed—or else his mama wouldn't
have anything to sit on!

Johnson didn't even have a magazine yet when he asked twenty
thousand of the insurance company's policyholders to pay two dollars each to subscribe to it. Around 3,000 of them did. That's how
he started *Negro Digest*, in 1942—it was inspired by *Reader's Digest*.
He took the best of what was happening with black folks around
the country and put it in the magazine. Inside of a year, the magazine had a circulation of 50,000.

Johnson's two biggest ideas were still to come, though. He decided he wanted to have a magazine to show black *and* white folks
that blacks did all the things everybody else did, from running
businesses to having beauty contests. (That shouldn't have been
news, but it was.) That magazine was *Ebony*, which he launched in
1945. At its height, it had a circulation of over two million. Today,
it's got a circulation of 1.27 million.

Then came *Jet*, which Johnson started in 1951. That was for
high-profile black people—politicians, athletes, socialites, entertainers. Black people could read that and have something to be
proud of—not just from history, but from what was going on right
then.

That was Johnson's fantastic contribution. All of it came through
his vision.

But he didn't stop there, either. He started a magazine for
kids called *Ebony Jr!* and another one called *African American Stars*.
And if that wasn't enough, his company published books, and he
bought two radio stations—he was the first black person in Chicago to own any kind of broadcasting company. Plus, in 1958, he
started the *Ebony* Fashion Fair. His wife, Eunice, ran it. Even today, most fashion and makeup companies don't put their products

out there with black folks in mind, and in 1958 most folks weren't even thinking about it. But Johnson was. The *Ebony* Fashion Fair turned into the biggest traveling fashion show on the planet, and since then, it has raised over $50 million for the United Negro College Fund and other charities.

In 1957, Johnson went on a goodwill tour of nine countries in Africa with Richard Nixon, who was vice president of the United States at the time. In 1961, President Kennedy made Johnson a special U.S. ambassador to Côte d'Ivoire after it became independent. In 1995, Bill Clinton gave him the Presidential Medal of Freedom. He got the Spingarn Medal from the NAACP in 1966.

Not bad for a boy growing up with no access to high school.

Earl Graves and the Founding of *Black Enterprise* Magazine

Black Enterprise magazine was started in 1970, and today it has almost four million readers. In 1973, the magazine started publishing an annual list of the top one hundred black-owned companies in America, which was the only way you'd have known there *were* a hundred black-owned companies in America, because if you'd waited for the *New York Times* or *USA Today* to tell you, you'd have been waiting till the cows came home.

Earl G. Graves started *Black Enterprise*.

Graves was born in 1935 and grew up in Brooklyn, but his grandparents came from Barbados. When black folks grow up outside the United States and don't have that slave mentality, they know they can do something, and Earl's grandparents passed that notion down to him. From early on, he thought like an entrepreneur. An entrepreneur says, "Find a need and fill it," and that's what Graves did.

When he was six years old, that little man was going out selling
Christmas cards. He probably would have made his fortune right
then, except his daddy would let him sell only to folks who lived
on the block. Earl Graves's folks believed in education, and Earl
himself could see how important it was, because his daddy couldn't
get a white-collar job since he had only a high school education. So,
Earl went to college, and he was a businessman there, too. At Morgan State University, in Baltimore, he realized that everybody and
his brother wanted flowers for Homecoming Week, so he made
a deal with two florists and sold flowers all over campus. Today,
Morgan State has a business school named after him.

After he graduated, he went back to Brooklyn and started selling real estate and doing work with the church. But what really
got his career going was when he got involved with politics. He
saw things changing for black folks in the 1960s, and he wanted
to be a part of it. See, nearly 100 years after emancipation is truly
when real progress was made concerning discrimination. In the
late Sixties and early Seventies more opportunities came along in
the corporate sphere, academia, and other areas. Blacks were being hired for more than menial labor and domestic work. It was a
time of serious growth. Earl Graves volunteered for the Democrats
in 1964, the year Lyndon Johnson won the presidency and Bobby
Kennedy was elected to the U.S. Senate from New York State.
That year, Kennedy threw Christmas parties for kids in all five
boroughs of New York City, and Graves signed up to organize the
one in Brooklyn. All the other parties had something wrong with
them—at one of them, somebody stole all the kids' toys!—but
when Kennedy got to the party in Brooklyn and saw a drum-and-
bugle corps and heard a full gospel choir singing, he turned to Earl
Graves and said, "Tell me your name again."

That's how Graves became an administrative aide on Bobby

Kennedy's staff. And that opened up a whole world of contacts. Graves met politicians, businesspeople, athletes, and celebrities. *That's* how you get somewhere in this world—meeting people.

When Kennedy was assassinated in 1968, Graves was shocked, but he had a lot of things he could do after that, because of all the folks he had met. He decided he wanted to be a consultant to black businesspeople. And what he did next tells you something: he went to Barbados, where his grandparents were from, and saw how black folks did business *there*—how black folks operated when they didn't have white folks and their own slave mentality getting in the way. And he brought that back here. At first, he was going to start a newsletter to go along with his consulting business, but a friend of his told him he needed to think bigger. That's how he started *Black Enterprise* magazine.

Graves worked like a dog to attract subscribers and advertisers to the magazine, and it worked. In its first year, the magazine sold $900,000 worth of ads, and it started turning a profit with its tenth issue. Its journalists would write about black businesses that the *Wall Street Journal, Fortune,* and *BusinessWeek* ignored. If you want to do business well, folks have to know that your business exists.

The Founding of *Essence* Magazine

Let's say I'm a black woman, and my son is living with me and talking all kinds of crazy stuff because he's on drugs. So, I want to see another side of black life that I can't see in my own house. That's what magazines like *Ebony, Jet,* and *Black Enterprise* are good for. And the same goes for the beauty magazine for black women, *Essence.*

In 1970, after so many things had changed for black folks, they weren't facing the same kind of challenges Johnson had had to deal with in 1945.

The magazine's first editor was Marcia Ann Gillespie, who held the job for ten years. Meanwhile, when the magazine started, a twenty-three-year-old woman named Susan Taylor, who hadn't even been to college, got the job as beauty editor. Taylor was something else: she had already started a company called Nequai Cosmetics, which sold beauty products for black women, so she knew her stuff. (She eventually got her college degree by going to night school in the 1980s.) When Marcia Ann Gillespie left, Susan Taylor became the editor of *Essence*, and the magazine really flourished under her. She wrote a monthly column for *Essence* called "In the Spirit," which talked about things like self-esteem, family, and health. She left in 2000, and there have been five editors since, all women. The magazine started out with a circulation of 50,000, and now it's over 1.5 million. And the readership is about four times that. *Essence* has branched out into other things, too: every year in New Orleans they have a music festival that draws almost half a million people. (Barack Obama went to it one year.) The festival they had in 2009 was in honor of Obama's inauguration, and Beyoncé headlined it.

That's how important that magazine is.

5

Running in Place, Embarrassing the Race

One of the things holding black
folks down: malt liquor.

When I look at baseball or football or basketball, I see
slavery all over again. The black person out in the
field with a football or a basketball—that ball is the
cotton. When you look at sports, who are the people they get to
play them? Poor folks and more specifically, usually poor black
folks. Meanwhile, the white boy is sitting on the bench with a clip-
board trying to act intelligent. Nothing has changed since slavery;
it's just moved to a higher order.

We're talking about a trillion-dollar industry, but where does
athletes' money go? What big companies have they got? They
don't have any, because they're nothing but athletes. Look at athletes and entertainers, black and white: athletes sign $100 million
contracts, but they don't have any money. They've got systems out
there that take it away. In that business, the money goes from a

father—let's say he's an accountant—to a big white entertainment manager like Joe Glaser, and it passes down through generations of a family. So, when you hit the sixth-generation accountant of that same family, that's who's wiping the athlete out financially, that's the person the athlete's or entertainer's money goes to. And if you're the athlete or entertainer, you don't know anything. You're scared. You start out poor, and your skills take you into another world, another life, and they tell you, "You have to do this, you have to do that, you have to do this other thing."

America doesn't use athletes for anything important. America's won nearly every war it's fought, and it didn't use entertainers or athletes. So, athletes and entertainers are just the thing to put people to sleep.

How come billionaire white folks don't have their children playing sports? Because nobody plays sports but a poor ignorant person. Why is that? Because it tears up the body. Think about that, man. With all the technical stuff they're doing now with sports medicine to help athletes heal faster, and rich folks *still* don't play games. A billionaire owns a *horse*, man, and has it trained to run until it can't run anymore. I've done some research on horses; a horse is one of the dumbest things on the planet, the only animal that will run into a barn that's on fire. And in some ways an athlete isn't much different.

This is how vicious the world of sports is: You live a better life, but that's just for a few minutes; that doesn't last any time at all. Also, they drug athletes up whenever they want to. (But when you go get some dope on your own, then it's called criminal.) All athletes get treated that way, but for black athletes, it's worse.

Look at Coach Bear Bryant at the University of Alabama. People asked him, "How come you got no black players?" He said, "I'll be dead in my grave 'fore I'll get a nigger." And then he started using some, and people said, "What happened?" and Bryant said, "Well, I wanted to win!" But there's no love there. None at all.

The great story, man, is about Woody Hayes, the football coach at Ohio State University. He would bring you in, cuss you out, and then hit you. One time, this black player said, "Coach Hayes, my daddy told me to tell you you'd better not hit me, and if you do, to whup yo' ass." Just like that. "I ain't comin' down here to be yo' boy. I'm coming down here to play football, and I know once I can't play football, I'm outta here." So, whenever that player messed up, Hayes would bring him in and have another black player stand next to him, and he'd cuss out *that other player* instead!

For black *women* it's worse still. There have been some great black female athletes, like the tennis player Althea Gibson, track-and-field stars Florence Griffith Joyner and Jackie Joyner-Kersee, and the tennis stars Venus and Serena Williams. Women are beginning to come out a little more, but it's still the same thing—not as bad, but it's still bad. We know more about Tiger Woods than the Williams sisters because he's a man. We know everything about him.

Tiger tried to say he wasn't black; he was "Caublasian"—meaning Caucasian, black, and Asian. Yeah, tell me another one. I got up on-stage and said, "Can you imagine Tiger Woods going to dinner at the White House with twelve powerful white boys, and when they leave they come out that back gate to Pennsylvania Avenue and somebody drives by and says, "Hit the ground, nigger!" I said, "Which one of them y'all think will drop to the ground?" The boys with him would be saying, "Tiger, what's wrong with you? Why you on the ground?"

For years, man, they convinced us that black people could run the short dashes because of our legs, but that it was white folk who could run the long distances. Sometimes when I perform, I say, "Any white dudes out there who are six foot ten inches? Come up on the stage." I say, "I'm five foot ten. Now stand next to me. My legs come to your chest." Black folks have long legs and short bodies. White folks have short legs and long bodies. Based on racist ideas, black people have been compared to apes and the like for as long as I can remember.

All I have to say is that gorillas have short legs and long bodies. If I took five gorillas, five white men, and five black men, which two groups have hair all over their bodies? The gorillas and the white men. If you go to the zoo and look at the gorilla family, they got lips thinner than razor blades, so how can they convince black folks that we look like gorillas? But they can.

In sports, the athlete is a *gladiator*: "Go in, fight those lions and those tigers, and we'll sit up in the stands and look." And the boxing thing is a sex hang-up. That's how the Man got his rocks off, looking at black folks fighting, beating each other to death.

But one reason that sports is *good* is that when one black person does it, he does it for *all of us*—for the ones who went to jail, for the ones who didn't have the training facilities, for the ones who didn't have good coaches.

The athletes in this next section are some of the ones who did it for all of us.

Satchel Paige and the Negro Baseball Leagues

In the United States, immigration was mostly an East Coast phenomenon. In the late 1800s and early 1900s, most immigrants arriving on American shores were largely coming into New York City. When they arrived at the Garden Castle Depot and later Ellis Island, they moved right into segregated communities. There was a Jewish ghetto, a Lithuanian ghetto, an Irish ghetto, and so on. But the game of baseball had an interesting way of bringing them all together. See, when folks went to baseball games, there was no specific seating areas for one group or another. That's why baseball was called America's game. You became an American at the ballpark. People from all over the world showed up at the ballpark as one unified body. But when they left, they returned to their Polish, Italian, and Russian ghettos. Baseball embraced America's melting pot, as long as it didn't include black folks.

Now, folks will say anything to make themselves feel better about getting older and dying:

"It's nothin' but a number."

"You're only as old as you feel."

"I'm a hundred fifty-nine years *young*."

Yeah. It might be nothing but a number, but if the number is over seventy and you're counting the years you've been on this earth, you're not exactly the Little Green Sprout. And do me a favor. If you ever hear me say, "I'm blankety-blank years young," hold a pillow over my face good and tight.

But that's all right. There are worse things than getting old. *Not* getting old, for one. And if there was one dude who made you believe you really were as young as you felt, it was the pitcher Satchel Paige.

Paige was born in Alabama in 1906. He started to pitch in reform school, where he spent five years beginning when he was thirteen. Now, if you know anything about Satchel Paige, you know that he had what they called a hesitation pitch. He had learned it as a boy: when he and his friends would pass a gang of mean older white boys, Satchel had to throw rocks and bricks to protect himself. He'd wind up that brick, but then hesitate while the other boy flinched and bent over. And when the white boy had made himself into a big fat target crouching there on the ground, Satchel would throw the brick and knock his brains out. That became the hesitation pitch when Paige started playing baseball. *Pow!*

After that, he pitched for over two decades in the Negro Leagues, before Major League Baseball was integrated. The "Negro" teams started forming in the 1880s, after black folks got left out of the Major Leagues. These were all-black teams, like the Homestead Grays and the Philadelphia Giants, but they didn't get good and organized until 1920, when the Negro National League was founded. I was shocked when I found out that the Negro Leagues in baseball made more money—I mean more money per player—than the white leagues. That's right. They made more money than Stan Musial and all the big boys. For one thing, they played twelve months out of the year—they didn't have nine months off where they could go drink and do any fool thing they wanted.

But back to Satchel Paige: You may have heard some Satchel Paige sayings. Like "How old would you be if you didn't know how old you were?" or "Don't look back; something might be gaining on you," or "Don't pray when it rains if you don't pray when the sun shines."

My favorite story about Satchel is this one: Sometimes the Negro teams would play the best white baseball team in the county, and the "Negroes" would wipe them out. Probably the greatest thing that came out of this, for me, was the story about Babe Ruth. Ruth set the home run record worldwide. (Nobody plays baseball but Americans and one or two other countries, but privileged folks can declare anything they do as being "worldwide.") The Babe was the home run king—he hit 714 homers, a record that stood for almost forty years, until a black man, Hank Aaron, broke it in 1974. (By the way, take a good look at a picture of Babe Ruth and tell me that that big, fat dude didn't have some black blood in him. It was a good thing he could hit, because he sure couldn't *run*. Look at some videos of him going around the bases after he hit a home run. If he had moved any slower, he would've been going backward.) So, in his day, Babe Ruth became *the* greatest star of any sport. So, now he's coming to St. Louis, where Satchel Paige is playing with the Browns, because the Negro League, which was run by white folks, would go into the big stadiums while the white team was on the road. Babe Ruth comes up to bat. Paige is pitching. Babe Ruth never hit a Satchel Paige pitch in his life, but now—*pow*! Ruth smacked the ball out of the stadium.

Satchel runs over to third base and starts trash-talking Ruth, saying, "You dirty dog, you, you'd better thank God for me." He said, "I let you hit that pitch." Why? "So the black folks in the stands would get to see what folks are going crazy over. I just wanted them to see. See, we had to turn away thousands of people who wanted to see you today. But for the ones who got in, I just wanted my people to see you and see what all the fuss is about. See if you ever hit me again in your life." And for the rest of that game, the Babe didn't get any part of a pitch Satchel threw. Now, that's loving your people. Oh man, you talk about humanity? Satchel Paige was saying: This isn't about me. This is about all the people who come to these games. Okay? After that, what is baseball? After that?

I was saying how Satchel Paige could make you believe you were as young as you felt. Here's what I'm talking about: After Jackie Robinson broke the color barrier, Satchel became Major League Baseball's oldest rookie—at forty-two. A baby could have been born when Satchel started playing ball, grown up to play ball himself, and found himself on the same team with that Methuselah of the Mound. Satchel pitched with the St. Louis Browns till he was within spitting distance of fifty. Any fifty-year-olds reading this, think about how your back felt the last time you stayed on your feet too long, and then think about Paige standing out there on that mound for nine-plus innings. And not just standing there, either: reaching way back, kicking that foot out like he'd learned to do in reform school, launching that fastball, and striking folks out.

Jack Johnson, Joe Louis, Max Schmeling, and King Kong

You'd have a tough time overstating how big Joe Louis was in his day. The heavyweight boxing championship—well, that was the nation's number one symbol of manhood. And for a black man to hold that title, which Louis did from 1937 to 1949—that meant something back then. He was the first black man to be the hero not just of black folks but of *all* Americans. One thing about Joe Louis was how easy he made it look. Next to him, the other guy in the ring always looked like he was trying to figure out how to fight, and Joe would just step over, like he was saying, "Here, let me show you"—and *whap, whap, ka-POW!*

Joe was born in Alabama in 1914, the next-to-last of eight kids. He had a speech problem when he was little, so he didn't talk a lot; even as champ, he wasn't known for talking that much. When he was twelve, his family moved to Detroit to get away from the Ku Klux Klan. Up there, he started boxing as a teenager and won just about every amateur championship there was before he turned pro, in 1934.

Joe won seventy fights in his pro career and lost only three times. The first time was the worst. Boy, you'd have to go back to slavery times to see black folks feeling as low as they felt the night that white German fighter Max Schmeling knocked out Joe Louis. June 1936, twelfth round. See, Schmeling had been studying Joe's style. One day, he said in that German accent that made him sound like every Nazi you ever saw in the movies, "I have seen something." Having studied the way Joe left himself open when he threw a punch, on that June night in 1936, Schmeling waited for that opening and went in for the kill. That's how he got Joe down.

Well, Joe wasn't about to let that happen twice. They fought again, in June 1938, a year after Joe had beat Jim Braddock to become the champ. In the rematch, Joe hit Schmeling so hard that the big German went *rolling* on the canvas. I never knew till I was grown that when Louis beat Schmeling, neither one of them was champ. I thought that when Max Schmeling beat Louis, he was the champion, and that Louis came back and beat Schmeling and became champ again. But it wasn't like that.

Now, because of Jack Johnson, the *first* black heavyweight boxing champion, and all the white women he went around with, for years a black man couldn't be heavyweight champ. White folks just wouldn't let it happen. So, when Louis was being groomed, his handlers said, "You can never do this, you can never do that"—if he won a fight, he couldn't hold his hands above his head, like every fighter today does. If he had whipped a white boy and then had the nerve to hold his hands up over his head, there'd probably have been a riot. Those hands of his could mess a man up in the ring, though.

And the way they did Joe Louis, man . . .

He boxed for a benefit—you know the story?—for the Army Emergency Relief. Didn't take a dollar of the purse, donated all to the charity, but he had to pay taxes on that whole purse. You hear me? So, even when you're doing what they want you to do, you still come up short.

But I was talking just now about Jack Johnson. When you think about what he was able to do, it's incredible. As hard as it was for Joe Louis to be a black boxing champion in the 1930s, how hard do you think it was for a black champion more than

twenty years *earlier* than that? During the same period that
white folks were getting so excited by the 1915 movie *Birth of a
Nation* that they were turning the lynching of black folks into a
national sport, a time when black folks risked their lives just by
leaving home in the morning, there's Jack Johnson, a son of two
former slaves, acting like he didn't care about *any* of it. That was
one bad brotha. At a time when you could go to jail or worse for
looking a white person in the eye, Jack Johnson would get in the
ring in front of thousands of white folks and beat those white
boys silly, trash-talking the whole time. Nobody could touch
him in the ring. He was dark-skinned, bald, muscular—*sleek*,
you hear me? Like a panther. Moved like one, too, just as quick
and smooth as you please. He went right on beating up those
white boys, and white people went crazy watching him do it,
but Jack Johnson didn't care.

He was born in 1878 in Galveston, Texas. His family was poor,
but everybody where he lived, black and white alike, was poor, so
it was like they were all in it together. Johnson would hang out
with white boys, and he never remembered any prejudice against
him. As a young man, he made his way to Dallas, where a man
he worked for turned him on to boxing. Johnson then turned pro
back in Galveston, in 1898. Ten years later he became the heavyweight champ when he knocked out Tommy Burns in Australia.
By then, he was used to beating up on white dudes.

But beating up white boxers was only half of it. Outside the
ring, Jack Johnson loved himself some white women. He'd get
all dressed up in his suit and hat, parading around with them,
until white folks were just about foaming at the mouth. He got
arrested in 1912 for violating the Mann Act, which said you
couldn't transport women across state lines for "immoral pur-

poses." The woman he was with wanted to be with him—she later married him—so the "immoral" part, as far as the authorities were concerned, was that she was white and he was black.

Even before that, white people were so desperate for a white man, *any* white man, to beat Jack Johnson that they hounded Jim Jeffries till he agreed to come out of retirement and fight again. Jeffries had become a farmer, and before Jack Johnson was through with him, he probably wished he had stayed on the farm. Now, these days, a long fight lasts for fifteen rounds, but back in those times, in the fifteenth round, things were just getting started. Boxers back then fought until somebody dropped. The Johnson-Jeffries fight, on July 4, 1910, was supposed to be *forty-five rounds*—in hundred-degree heat. But Johnson only needed fifteen, and it wasn't much of a fight even for most of that. Jeffries said after it was over that even at his prime, he couldn't have touched Jack Johnson.

In 1915, they finally found a white boy to beat Johnson: Jess Willard. Johnson never fought for the heavyweight title again. (He was beating Willard for twenty-some rounds, till he got tired. Think about that. If Johnson had come along later in history, when there was the fifteen-round limit, he probably would never have lost the championship.) Even after he lost, he stayed on people's minds a good long time. Because look here:

In 1933, the movie *King Kong* came out. Think about this, now. A big, dark giant ape kidnaps a white woman and takes her with him up the Empire State Building, a building that looks like the biggest penis on the planet. When he gets to the top, white men send in airplanes, and Kong gets shot till he falls to his death. Why New York? There are no bananas growing in New York, and Lord knows there are hardly any trees. But right down the street from the Empire State Building is the boxing capital of the world, Madison Square Garden. If you can't read the coded message in that, you don't know what's happening.

Now, who do you think that movie was really about?

Jesse Owens and the Real God

One day, the universe stepped in and said, "Okay, we're gonna take a black man from the belly of Lake Erie on the East Side of Cleveland named Jesse Owens, born in Alabama in 1913, and we're going to find another black man on the West Side of Chicago, Ralph Metcalfe, born in Georgia in 1910. And those two will go to the Olympics."

Jesse Owens wasn't but in high school in 1933 when he tied the world record of 9.4 seconds in the 100-yard dash at the National High School Championship in Chicago. Then he went to Ohio State University and won eight NCAA championships in 1935 and 1936.

Then came the 1936 Olympics, in Hitler's Berlin. The dirty dog who ran the U.S.-based Amateur Athletic Union, the AAU, hated Jews and blacks. But Metcalfe and Owens went on to the Olympics because the AAU knew that Owens would win the 100-meter sprint, and it knew this for a reason the average person didn't know: there was no rule that you had to participate in the preliminaries to qualify for the Olympics. There were no technicalities to get in Owens's way, so the AAU knew he'd probably set a world record. They knew that he might not even finish in the 220 meters because of the preliminaries, which had given him problems.

Well, sure enough, Jesse won the 100 meters in world-record time.

The reason Jesse and Metcalfe became millionaires was because of something that happened two days later. That was when Jesse had to do the long jump. The organizers knew that in all his Big Ten competitions, which were held every year, Jesse was disqualified in 98 percent of his long jumps because his foot went over that white line—what they call the takeoff board. So, the story Jesse told about what happened next makes you understand the real God. Some say it didn't happen this way, but this is the way Jesse told it. A German, speaking English, walked up to him and said, "My brother, your gyroscope in your head, your inner ear, messes up your equilibrium, and that's why you're disqualified so much of the time, because you step over the takeoff board." A German who spoke English said that to him. And not just any German. This was Luz Long, Jesse's competitor in the long jump.

So, the rule is: if your foot goes over the takeoff board, you're disqualified. But it didn't say Jesse couldn't move the line back five inches. They moved it back, and Jesse jumped out of the long jump pit. A new world's record! That wouldn't have happened had that German not told him that. Now, what are the odds of coming to the Olympics and finding an English-speaking German? That's the universe at work.

Jesse Owens won four gold medals at the Berlin Olympics—for the long jump, the 100 meters, the 200 meters, and the 4 x 100 relays. He ran in the relays partly because of Avery Brundage, who was in charge of the U.S. Olympic teams. The Germans told Brundage to get two Jews, Marty Glickman and Sam Stoller, off the U.S. 4 x 100 relay team. And he did. That's when officials came to Jesse Owens and Ralph Metcalfe and said to both of them, "Y'all need to run the relay 'cause the Jews ain't running." Jesse and Ralph said that the Olympic officials should just cancel the event, but they didn't.

Jesse Owens said about Glickman, "I don't know where he came from. I don't care how far a man was ahead of him, when you came off that turn, Glickman would chase you down. That's the kind of runner Marty Glickman was. When he came off that turn, man, I don't care where you were, Glickman was going to get you."

So, the two of them, Glickman and Stoller, came to Jesse Owens and Ralph Metcalfe and said, "Man, we'll handle this when we get back home." Both of them were crying, but they told Jesse and Ralph, "Hey, man, you know winning the relay is not about how fast you can run. It's all about the exchange of the stick. We haven't practiced that." They said, "When you run, let Metcalfe start off first." That's what they did, and when the relay race was over, the United States had a new world record. That's how Jesse Owens got four world records. That's what sports is about: when something else steps in, and an athlete becomes something other than just a gladiator.

Because of what happened in 1936, Jesse Owens is probably the most famous runner of all time. Ralph Metcalfe didn't do too bad, either. Go watch some footage of Jesse running in that Olympics. You'll see what you see when you watch the best athletes in the world at work, like Joe Louis, Muhammad Ali, Michael Jordan— somebody making it look easy. The way Jordan could fly to the basket for a slam dunk like he had wings, the way Ali could move his head out of the way of a lightning-fast punch like it was the most natural thing in the world, the way Joe Louis could walk up to a fit, muscular man and leave him on the canvas wondering what just happened—that's how Jesse ran: so easy. All those runners straining and puffing behind him, and in front of them, there's Jesse, in perfect form, looking relaxed, like he's out for a quick jog on a nice Sunday morning, except he's moving faster than any human being on the planet. And he's doing that while one of the biggest white supremacists in all of history is gazing down on him. That's how to keep your cool and your dignity, man, in the face of the worst the world can dish out.

Over forty years later, when Jesse was lying in the hospital, dying of lung cancer, his wife came to see me. She said to me, "Greg, he's acting so evil." I said, "The man is about to leave his money and his woman back here for somebody else. Lady, you'd better find you some combat boots and dress up in long ugly clothes next time you go see him." And she did, and she told me, "It worked. It worked. He just hugged me."

You know what it's like, man, to see your wife when you know, and she knows, that you're dying? See your wife stroll in there with the latest threads on? And you know that when you're gone, she's going to be with somebody else? That's hard to handle. And it's not like he was a philosopher. The man was just an athlete, that's all.

Jackie Robinson

In 1947, when Jackie Robinson went to play for the Brooklyn Dodgers, he became the first black player in Major League Baseball in modern times. Well, everybody knows that. But what people may *not* know is that he had to be more than just an athlete. That's the only way he could have done what he did. The way he carried himself, talking the way every mother would like her son to talk— it was because he knew that when he was in public, *he was all of us.* With every play he made in the Major Leagues, he was representing black people. Most athletes today think that it is all about them. Do you think Darryl Strawberry, Len Bias, Dennis Rodman, or Lamar Odom felt that they had a community to represent? Every time some racist called Jackie Robinson a nigger, and Jackie went on about his business like he hadn't heard it, staying calm and keeping his dignity, he was representing black people—and he knew it.

It wasn't that he didn't feel anything. But he had to hold those feelings inside himself in order to accomplish what he did as an athlete. And it was keeping them inside that finally killed him. The thing that let him succeed in the Majors was the thing that finally took him away. He held all that in so other blacks could come through behind him. What a hell of a price to pay. Today, black athletes are still called nigger or booed on the regular.

Jackie's life was one long struggle. He was born in 1919 in Georgia, the youngest of five children in a family of sharecroppers. Jackie's father left the family a year after Jackie was born, and Jackie's mother took the kids with her to California. They were the poorest family on the block, and the only black one, and if you think their neighbors gave them a hard time, you're right. So, what Jackie later faced from racists in the Major Leagues was nothing new to him.

Jackie was one of the only black athletes in his high school, too, but if they gave him a hard time, it didn't mess with his playing. It would be faster to list the sports he *wasn't* good at than to list the ones where he was a star—then again, it wouldn't, because you'd have to think hard to name a single sport he wasn't good at. He got letters in baseball, track, basketball, and football, and he was a champion tennis player. He went to Pasadena Junior College and then to UCLA, where he lettered in those first four sports and became the first one there to do it. That young brother was something else. Turned out he was a little bit *too* much for the military when he got drafted in 1942. They found out he wasn't taking their racist crap. He became an officer, second lieutenant, but that didn't stop a civilian bus driver from trying to send him to the back of the bus. When Jackie refused, the driver called the military police, and they came and took him away and court-martialed him. He got acquitted, though, and left the service with an honorable discharge.

After he got out of the army, he coached at a school in Texas and then played for a year in the Negro Baseball League, as a shortstop for the Kansas City Monarchs. He was with them when Branch Rickey came looking for him, and then everything changed.

Rickey was president and general manager of the Brooklyn Dodgers, and he was set on hiring a black player to integrate baseball. Now, Jackie wasn't necessarily the best player in the Negro League. Most folks thought Satchel Paige and Josh Gibson were better. Hell, Jackie wasn't even the best athlete in his own *family*; he had a brother who was better than he was. But his brother was hot-headed, while Jackie knew how to stay cool when he had to. Branch Rickey and Jackie Robinson had a famous conversation about how Jackie couldn't react when people gave him a hard time for playing in the Majors:

Jackie said, "Are you looking for a Negro who is afraid to fight back?"

Branch Rickey answered him: "I'm looking for a Negro with guts enough *not* to fight back."

And there was plenty not to fight back *against*. Jackie played second base, and some of the opposing players would come sliding in with their cleats up, trying to draw blood. One time, Jackie ended up with a seven-inch gash in his leg. Players on the opposing teams would also holler "nigger" at him from the dugout. Jackie didn't say a word. But he had his revenge. He played so well that he won Rookie of the Year in 1947, played in All-Star Games for six straight years beginning in 1949, and played in six World Series. And in 1962, he made the Baseball Hall of Fame. The whole time he played, he was as cool as you please. He gave the civil rights leaders who came along later a model to follow—showed them how to stay calm while all kinds of crazy stuff was happening around them.

While Jackie was staying calm, other people around him were

changing. Even some of his white teammates initially weren't too crazy about having him on the team. But when they went on the road and saw what he had to go through just because he was black, they started to think a little differently. "We'd go to St. Louis on the bus, and poor Jackie had to go to another hotel"—that's from Eddie Stanky, who was on the Brooklyn Dodgers with Jackie. "That's pretty hard to live with. But it never changed his personality or his thoughts about the game. When that game started, that first pitch, he was all ball player and all man."

Jackie played for ten years and had a successful career after that, too. He became the first black vice president of Chock Full O' Nuts. But his baseball years, and keeping all that emotion inside him, took their toll on Jackie. That's the price he paid. That's why he got sugar diabetes and just about went blind. He wasn't but fifty-three when he died of a heart attack, in 1972. That was the sacrifice he made for his people.

Muhammad Ali Beats Sonny Liston

Muhammad Ali was one bad brotha. He was so bad that the Mob could never make him throw fights. They had to make the people he was *fighting* throw them.

In 1964, in Miami Beach, Ali beat Sonny Liston and became the champion. He was still known by his birth name, "Cassius Clay," then. But the day after he beat Liston, he announced to the world that his name would henceforth be Cassius X, because "Clay" was a slave name. Then, later, he became Muhammad Ali. The heavyweight boxing champion of the world was a Muslim, and there was nothing anybody could do about it! And because he was the champion, the networks had to interview him, but Ali would say, "Till we talk about Allah, you can't interview me." And every time he fought, they gave him time to talk about Allah. Nobody had ever seen anything like it—or like him.

But, we don't see the hurt behind it. Years later, old folks would sit there watching Tiger Woods and be just as happy as they could be. He was larger than Muhammad Ali. White folks told blacks to be scared of the Muslims, and they were. But my grandmother stopped eating pork for a black man in another religion that she would never join—that's how proud she was of Ali. No Christians ever did that for somebody in another religion. Stop eating certain things because this black man, whom white folks told us to hate, said so.

Sonny threw the second fight with Ali, in 1965, but that's not saying Ali *couldn't* fight. He could fight like nobody's business. Sonny was built like a bull, but Ali was long and lean and *fast*.

In that first fight, from the first round, Sonny was throwing punches at Ali's face. The punches would almost land, and then, all of a sudden, Ali's face just wasn't *there*—he'd slip it to the side at the last moment and then throw that left hand. Sometimes it looked like he made his whole body disappear before Sonny could hit it. Ali had those long arms—he had *reach*. He'd hold his guard just as low as you please, tempting Sonny to swing at that pretty face, and then Sonny would miss, and Ali would pound him with that left—*whap!*

In the third round of that first fight, Ali started pounding Sonny's head *good*. But Sonny wasn't ready to give up, not yet. He kept charging forward, like the bull he was, giving Ali some good body shots, but for every one he landed to the body, he missed two to Ali's head, what with Ali bobbing that head this way and that. In the fourth round, Sonny landed a decent hook to Ali's face—he was trying—but mostly Ali slipped every punch Sonny threw.

Still, Ali ran into trouble in that fourth round, because the stuff Sonny's corner men were using on *his* cuts got into *Ali's* eyes. You could see it when Ali was in his corner between the fourth and fifth rounds: he was blinking like crazy. When Ali came out in the fifth round, he couldn't half see, and Sonny started pounding away. Ali could still dance, though, and he'd put that left glove in Sonny's face and just hold it there, taunting him, till Sonny'd get so mad he'd swing and miss, just like they say in baseball—*a swing and a miss.*

Ali survived the round, and by the next round, he could see again. That's when he started putting together combinations— and I'm talking about some combinations that could've opened a *safe.* Beat Sonny so bad he wouldn't come out of his corner for the seventh round. And that's how Ali became champ.

And the Mob made sure he *stayed* champ. Man, Sonny was so mad he had to throw that second fight, but the way he did it was brilliant. He didn't waste time: he did it in the first round. Sonny was at the center of the ring the whole time, and Ali was dancing around him like Sonny was a maypole. And then came what the white boys called the "phantom punch."

Phantom punch—that was some BS. Go look at the video. Sonny fell down without even being *hit.* And the folks didn't miss a beat: "Oh, Ali got him with that phantom punch," so fast the human eye couldn't see it, and the videotape couldn't capture it, no matter how many times you slowed the thing down.

That's what happens when white folks control everything, and then we pick up what they say and we run with it, like it's from Moses coming down off old Mount Sinai. And nobody checks it!

But Ali—even though he could *fight* like a demon, he had the heart of a child, so loving and kind. Like a child-man, so simple and kind. If you took him to your house and your grandma was sick, that man would stay there till nine o'clock. It was just his kindness, his niceness. You never saw anybody as kind as Ali. And why did he lose his money? Well, contributions to the Nation of Islam weren't tax deductible because the government called it a hate group. So, the money Ali gave the Nation didn't count. Bob Hope could give a billion dollars as a tax write-off, but not Ali. But Ali just kept doing what he was doing. He had a large family and generous Ali took care of them all. He couldn't get over it when he was invited to Harvard, Yale, and MIT—and he had barely finished high school! He was just so thrilled and happy, like a little boy.

He was born in 1942 in Louisville, Kentucky. He started boxing when he was twelve, and it wasn't long before he decided he wanted to do it for a living. No wonder: the boy could *fight*. He won half a dozen state championships and got a gold medal at the Olympics in Rome in 1960. To a black boy from Louisville back then, going to Rome must have seemed like going to the moon. Before he was done, though, people the world over knew who he was.

Everybody who has success, including Jesus, has had to move from *here* to *there*. In other words, nobody starts where he's supposed to be. You start at the wrong place, and then you move over *there*, where things happen. So, for Ali—have I told the story about Ali and the bike? When he was growing up in Louisville, his dad gave him a bike for his birthday, and the first day he went riding on that bike, somebody stole it. Ali panicked. He ran around looking for that bike, scared to go home. After a while, he went around the corner to the police station to report it, mad as a wet hen, threatening to beat up whoever had taken the bike. The cop he talked to also ran a boxing gym. When Ali went in and said, "Did anybody see a bike in there? Somebody stole my bike," the cop who owned the gym said, "When you get through and find it, come back and I'll teach ya how to fight." A nice story. And it started because Ali was looking for his bike!

So, when you stop and think about that: how did that happen? I mean, maybe if it hadn't been for that, he would have been just another trifling dude walking down the street, never having any idea he would one day go to Harvard and Yale to *speak*, go all over the world, talking to parliaments. Why? Because of a bike.

As great a boxer as Ali was, what people forget is that he spent three of the best years of his career outside the ring, after he refused to join the military during the Vietnam War and got stripped of the title he'd won from Liston. His thing was, why should he go over there and fight the yellow man, who'd never done a thing to him, all for the benefit of the white man, who'd raped and killed his ancestors? He said, "No Vietcong ever called me nigger." People ate that stuff up. He was a hero. A different kind from Joe Louis, but a hero just the same.

And he was *funny*. The way he'd talk about other fighters had you cracking up.

When he could fight again, he fought Joe Frazier. Lost the first time; won the second two. That third one—you never saw a more brutal fight in your life. How he and Joe survived that, I don't know. And the year before that, Ali had done what nobody thought he could do: he whupped George Foreman. Used the rope-a-dope on him till Foreman was so tired he couldn't see straight, and then Ali went to work. Ever see a clip of Foreman falling to the canvas at the end of that fight? All that was missing was somebody yelling, "Timberrrrrr!"

No matter how good you are, though, you can't fight the men Ali fought and not suffer some damage. That Parkinson's he had was from getting hit by the toughest dudes on the planet. By the time he died in 2016, Ali was so quiet you wouldn't have known this was the same man who used to make up rhymes about his opponents. But go back and look at those fights. That brotha could fight like nobody else. He shook up the world, all right. Nothing can change that.

Ali was a disciple of Elijah Muhammad, the head of the Nation of Islam. Elijah Muhammad lived around the corner from me. I used to love to go talk to him. One time, he said to me, "When are you going to join the mosque?" He said I was more like a Muslim than a Muslim. I said, "Let me tell you something, old man. Anytime you see me on TV, I'm just trying to make black folks laugh, make white folks laugh. That's all I'm trying to do. Make niggers glad and white folk to be sad—I'm not trying to join nothing." Another thing about Elijah Muhammad: you never ate bean soup until you ate some that came out of *his* house.

Anyway, I just liked to listen to him, because he did something nobody else did. He couldn't talk, couldn't speak; he was an ignorant somebody. But he rented all-white radio stations on Saturday and put his message out there. Every Saturday. He was like Daddy Grace that way.

But I was talking about Ali. I went to his funeral, and a guy said to me, "What do you think?" I said, "I don't know." I told him there are no words in the English language that can describe what we lost when Ali died.

I mean, you had to be around him, man. Like I said, he was like a child: happy. When I was running across the country, Ali would come out and see me between fights. One time, the girl who was doing PR for Muhammad hurt her leg, so we took her to the hospital. Word got around that Dick Gregory was in the lobby. So, this woman who was dying from cancer—an old black-hating white woman; you can't look as old as her and not hate black people—she said, "Mr. Gregory, they tell me Ali, Ali, he's coming back here after the fight in Germany. You think he'll come see me?"

Well, I *wasn't* thinking, because if you're running fifty miles a day, like I was then, and Ali was coming back four days later, my mind would have been two hundred miles away. But somehow, I remembered the white lady's request, and I took Ali by the hospital. He walked to the woman's bed, picked her up, kissed her on the mouth, and told her, "I'm the greatest. Tell me you love me." We got there at ten o'clock in the morning. At six o'clock that night he was still there, doing his little jokes for her. That was Ali. The whole humanity piece, you know?

Harry Edwards and the 1968 Olympics

Harry Edwards is a black sociologist, born in 1942. He studies the experiences of black athletes, and he works to recruit blacks for executive positions in sports. In 1969, Edwards wrote a book called *The Revolt of the Black Athlete*. He was an athlete himself: discus thrower on the San Jose State University track team. Maybe the thing people know him most for, though, is what happened in 1968, at the Olympics in Mexico City. Tommie Smith, a black runner, won the gold medal in the 200-meter event. Another young brother, John Carlos, won the bronze. When they were on the podium after having received their medals, with the "The Star-Spangled Banner" playing, instead of doing what everybody else does—just stand there looking like they can't believe they're really at the Olympics—these two brothers raised their fists, in protest of all the human rights abuses happening around the world, including to black folks.

Well, Harry Edwards was the one who pulled that together. Their gesture was part of his Olympic Project for Human Rights.

In 1964, the Amateur Athletic Union was holding Olympic trials at Public School Stadium in St. Louis, where I'm from. I said, "Wow." I was in San Francisco at the time, performing at the nightclub the hungry i. But when I heard about the trials, I said, "I'm gonna fly back to St. Louis, catch that midnight flight, and picket the trials with a sign asking Negroes to boycott the 1964 Olympics until we get civil rights legislation." This was so important that I went there with my picket sign, but black folks just looked the other way. Some white folks spat at me, and some others said, "You Communist bastard." So, I got back on the plane, and you want to talk about feeling low—I was feeling so *bad*. I just couldn't believe that people didn't care about something this critical. But what's important to you is not important to me. What's important to you is, you're going to make the team and finally get that girl to go out with you. So, I got back on the plane, depressed. They couldn't bring me whiskey fast enough.

Now it's four years later, 1968. Tommie Smith and John Carlos do their thing at the Olympics, and Dr. Harry Edwards writes a book, and he says, "Everybody asked me how'd I get the idea." And he said, "Well, it was Dick Gregory." He said, "I live in East St. Louis, across the bridge from St. Louis, Missouri. One day when I was in high school, my daddy says. 'I'm gon' take y'all to see the Olympic Trials. It's at Public School Stadium.' And I saw Dick Gregory with a picket sign. And that's where I got the idea."

After I heard that, I traveled around the world, and I saw those raised fists everywhere I went—a sign of solidarity. I kind of meditated on the real God and said, "Amen. Thank you. Sometimes I forget that I plant the turnips but it's your sunshine. It's your rain that waters the crops." That had never been brought home to me like that before. Nothing I could have done that day in 1964 could've had that much effect, but what those *athletes* did went all over the world.

Well, wouldn't you know it: America sent Smith and Carlos home *that same day*, disgraced. The *New York Times*, the world press, they all said, "Who are these niggers and why'd they interrupt our game?" But then the universe turned around, and those brothers became a symbol that ordinary people embraced, that ordinary people could have. But Jesus, what those two went through trying to make a living after all that. I mean, they did all right—Carlos played football, both of them became coaches, and Smith became a professor—but they're really not seen as the heroes they are. And the suffering they had to go through, getting accused of drug use, before they were lifted up to their rightful place. And they're *still* not there, because when you think about what they did, you have to ask, how come they're not talked about like Rosa Parks?

How can something happen that's so big and that moves people so much, and yet most people don't know anything about these two brothers? Somebody'd think they were born when they raised their fists and died right after. How'd they happen to go to San Jose? As good as they were, how did they end up there? And Harry Edwards—how come we don't know more about his daddy, who took him to the Olympic trials? Who was his mother? Somebody's got to tell the world how important this was and how it happened. These people are our heroes, you hear me?

Their story is another example of the universe at work—just like the story of Rosa Parks. She always said that had she known who the driver was that day, she would never have gotten on that bus—and the Montgomery bus boycotts might not have happened. The whole thing turned on something as little as that. With Tommie Smith and John Carlos, it was same: down to the universe. Had Harry Edwards not seen me with that picket sign that one day, he might never have come up with the idea for the Olympic demonstration and those two black fists might never have come to represent solidarity all over the world.

Tiger Woods

Now, I don't want to say *every* father should be out there pushing his kids to do music and sports while they're still in diapers, but, man, look what it did for Michael Jackson and Tiger Woods.

Tiger's daddy—who, by the way, was the funniest dude I've ever met, man—he started teaching him when Tiger was a little bitty tot. He told me about Tiger: "God owed me that little punk, with all them other triflin' children He gave me. I deserved Tiger."

The world had never seen a golfer like Tiger Woods before. Tiger was born in late 1975, started playing golf almost before he could talk, turned pro at twenty, and won the Masters Tournament in 1997. Walked away with almost half a million dollars.

And he wasn't half done yet. Look at what this young brother went on to do. What Joe Louis and Muhammad Ali were to boxing; what Langston Hughes was to poetry; what Louis Armstrong, Duke Ellington, Billie Holiday, and Charlie Parker were to jazz; what Satchel Paige and Jackie Robinson were to baseball—this man was to golf. He won the Masters three more times, won the U.S. Open three times, won the British Open three times, won the PGA Championship *four* times, and in 2001 he had all four of those championships at the *same* time. He became PGA Player of the Year almost more times than you can count, he got paid to do so many commercials you couldn't turn on your TV or open a magazine without seeing his mug, and in 2009 he became the first athlete to top a billion dollars in earnings. No wonder white supremacy put that man in their gun sights.

What was almost more amazing than all that: he got black folks interested in golf. Televised golf started at noon on Sunday, and black folks started going to the 7:00 a.m. church service so they could be home and cooking and ready to look at their boy. The earlier services grew so fast that nobody could believe it. They didn't have money for all the early services they needed so folks could get home on time. So, they kept having seven o'clock, eight o'clock, ten o'clock services. (Old black people know that God's at only the eleven o'clock service.) Black women loved Tiger, because he was the successful son they'd never had.

He was the one who could do this: He wasn't too dark; he spoke proper English. Black folks loved it. And nothing crushed them more than when that scandal happened. Wow. Black folks didn't know how white supremacy worked. Tiger had to win four more majors to tie Jack Nicklaus, five to be all-time champion. So, supremacists wanted to take him down. I can't prove it, but I'd be willing to bet they made a deal with him: "You want to go to jail for twenty years for violating the Mann Act with that girl, young-blood? No? Okay, you get out there and let the whole world see something happened to your back." Next thing we know, in 2014, he's having back surgery, and his game hasn't been the same since. That's what it's about.

He didn't know that the white folks coming to see him play in the majors didn't love him—he didn't know that until he had to get out of golf for a while, and the ticket sales went down 50 percent, because 50 percent of them were hoping to see him get beaten. But when you think people love you, and you ignore all the stuff that's happening? You miss what's really going on.

What did he go through, man, knowing he's smarter than most presidents but he can't be one? And even all the stuff he did—we're not going to hear about it. For example, the people who probably hired him as a consultant? (I don't know if they did or not, but that's what they normally do: "We'd like for you to say what you think about this. What do you think about that?" Then, if you're Tiger, you have to go home and see that thing you consulted about turn into a billion-dollar empire.) Well, Tiger double-crossed these black folks. They didn't know he never finished Stanford. And think about how hurt those black folks were after they had changed their church schedules for him! Then they find out he's just a low-down dog—all that adultery and the rest of it, when it came out that he had cheated on his wife with more than a hundred women. When he got out of golf—well, black folks were hurt. It made them hurt inside.

What really caused his downfall, though, was just that supremacists had to stop him from catching up to Jack Nicklaus. Old black folks lived just to see that. They didn't care anything about the damn golf—they just wanted to see a black man like Tiger succeed. Now they were looking at Tiger and seeing what white folks had done to him. Old black folks, they just said, "Humph." That's all they could say. "He was like my son. If I had to draw a perfect young black man, it would be just like him."

What happened to Tiger? What did it do to Grandma? What did it do to Grandpa? It hurt them. Because Tiger had given them a sense of dignity they'd never had.

Epilogue: Last Thoughts

Black people at our best: fierce when we have to be,
creating beauty when we have a chance.

On White Supremacy

The whole game that's being played on us black folks is really
about white supremacy. Even most *white* folks don't understand
white supremacy.

When I was a little boy, black folks tried to get me scared of
racist, redneck, nigger-hating old crackers, snuff-dipping, can't-
read, can't-write folks. Now, when I was nine years old, I said to
my brother, "Since when do those types of folks run things?" Our
problem has never been a man who can't read or write and is full
of hate. Our problem has been the president of Harvard, Yale,
MIT, and General Motors; it has been executives at pharmaceu-
tical companies who put out all kinds of bad medicine and don't
go to jail when they get caught, who have to pay but don't have to
admit they did anything wrong.

White supremacy *works.* The world is overwhelmingly nonwhite, but whites control the whole world. That's why, when even white folks see unidentified flying objects, people with white supremacy behind them will say, "Shut up, you didn't see anything." Because once you admit that there's somebody in the universe other than you, white supremacy goes out the window, doesn't it? Organized religion as we know it goes out the window, doesn't it? My grandmother doesn't have space in her head to believe there could be a Baptist on Mars. Worst of all, in the view of white supremacists, if we start to think we're not alone in the universe, then white supremacy doesn't mean a thing, because we would all become *earthlings*. There wouldn't be a Memphis or a Chicago or an America or a Russia or a China or an Africa—we would be *Earth people*. This is what this thing is about.

When you stop and think about all the trickery that goes into maintaining white supremacy, it blows your mind. People say, "Why are black folks so violent?" Here's one answer: malt liquor. Did you know that you can't buy malt liquor in a white neighborhood? Go to a white neighborhood and try to buy it; see if you can find any. Why are white beer companies making beer for black folks that they're not selling to white folks? Because they put a thing in it called manganese. Once you get enough manganese, you'll kill your mama. Now, the body needs manganese, but once you get too much, watch out.

Then there's pollution. Here's something from the *New York Daily News*, from Thursday, May 29, 1997: "Crime linked to pollution. Polluted water can cause brain damage that turns ordinary people into violent criminals." Now do you see why people with money buy bottled water? The researcher was Roger Masters of Dartmouth College, a brilliant scientist. He compared crime figures from the FBI with information on industrial discharges—in other words, pollution. First of all, nobody tells you that the FBI is keeping statistics on homicides caused by pollution. There's a relationship between lead exposure and homicide, yet they've got black folks reduced to such nothings that we believe the crime situation is *our* fault. Masters studied industrial discharges of lead and manganese and found a link between pollution levels and murder, assault, and robbery. Counties with the highest pollution levels have a crime rate that's triple the nation's average. Yet they make us believe that crime is a black thing.

Anytime you accept injustice, you become unjust. Anytime you peacefully coexist with filth, you become filthy. And when that happens, you start doing this stuff to *yourself*. Think about people in Jamaica: they're *super* black over there. Do you know a huge killer of young folks in Jamaica, even as you're reading this? I'm not talking about crack cocaine or drive-by shootings or automobile accidents. I'm talking about *bleaching cream*. A huge killer of women in China is bleaching cream. That's what Hollywood movies do with white supremacy. She's got to look *white*. Did you know that in New Orleans they still have brown bag parties? What's that, you ask? You and I go to a party, and when we get to the door, there's a brown bag hanging down from the ceiling, and if our skin is darker than the brown bag, we can't go in.

Here's a finding that came out of UCLA: "African-Americans and Caucasians have similar emotional brain activity when seeing African-Americans, psychiatrists find." These are scientific data; this isn't pimp talk. What they do is take a hundred white folks and, for six weeks, run them through a program, figuring out which people they like and which ones they don't like—not which *races*, but which *people*. When they're done with that, they perform brain scans on the hundred people, and their brain activity shows up on a big TV screen. Then they flash pictures of the people the participants said they liked: their mothers and other people close to them. And the researchers can see on the screen the brain movements that correspond to happiness. Then they show the subjects a picture of a black man. Well, 64 percent of white folks damn near jump through their skulls when they see it. The white folks weren't even aware of having that reaction. Now, they do the same experiment with a hundred black folks. When they showed *them* a black man, 63 percent of them had *the same reaction*. That's why they concluded that blacks and whites have similar emotional brain activity when seeing African Americans. This is a scientific finding. But we think we can peacefully coexist with filth and it doesn't affect us.

This is what white supremacy has done to us.

Now how do we start undoing that?

Acknowledgments

I have many special people to thank.

To my wife Lil, the real Dick Gregory: What you have sacrificed for me, our children and the planet is beyond words. You are the reason that I'm still here. Thank you. I love you.

To my siblings: Ron, Garland, Delores, Pauline, and (Presley). Before the world was ever introduced to Dick Gregory, you helped to love and nurture a young boy named Richard. Thank you.

To my children: Michele, Lynne, Satori, Paula, Zenobia, Gregory, Miss, Christian, Ayanna and Yohance. Ten beautiful and brilliant human beings. Thank you for being a part of this phenomenal journey. You were literally born into the Movement. Thank you for getting it. I love you.

To my grandchildren, always remember that greatness is in your DNA. You are the continuum of this legacy. Granddad loves you.

Clifford Thompson: What a brother, what a fine human being. I want to say thank you for helping me to pull this all together and get my words on paper. It was a fabulous journey we embarked on and I enjoyed every minute of it.

Tracy Sherrod: Few people understand how important the relationship between writer and publisher is. Tracy you are a blessing and a treasure. You had the original vision for this book and saw it through its completion. I am certain this project could not and would not have happened without you. I am eternally grateful for your service and equally happy to call you my friend.

Regina Brooks: When one has written as many books as I have, you get to know a lot of literary agents. Hats off to one of the finest ones I know. You were with me from day one of this project. Thank you for bringing this team together and being a catalyst for getting this book done.

Attorney Ricky Anderson & Attorney Rosalind Ray: to two of the finest legal minds I know. One part art, another part deal. Thank you both for outstanding representation. Both of you have my back and I truly appreciate that.

Christian Gregory: Family and business do not always mix; however, having you as my business manager has been an absolute blessing. Thank you for your intellect, thank you for your love and thank you for the laughter. I love you, son.

About the Author

RICHARD "DICK" CLAXTON GREGORY was an African American comedian, civil rights activist, and cultural icon who first performed in public in the 1950s. He is on Comedy Central's list of "100 Greatest Stand-Ups" and was the author of fourteen books, most notably the bestselling classic *Nigger: An Autobiography*. A hilariously authentic wisecracker and passionate fighter for justice, Gregory remains one of the most prized comedians of our time. He and his beloved wife, Lil, have ten kids.